THE
LIVERPOOL FC
QUIZ BOOK

THE
LIVERPOOL FC
QUIZ BOOK

COMPILED BY
MARC WHITE

FOREWORD BY
TOMMY SMITH

JOHN BLAKE

Published by John Blake Publishing Ltd
3 Bramber Court, 2 Bramber Road,
London W14 9PB, England

www.johnblakepublishing.co.uk

First published in paperback in 2009

ISBN 978-1-84454-662-6

British Library Cataloguing-in-Publication Data:
A catalogue record for this book is available from the British Library.

Design by www.envydesign.co.uk

Printed and bound in Great Britain
by CPI Bookmarque, Croydon CR0 4TD

1 3 5 7 9 10 8 6 4 2

Papers used by John Blake Publishing are natural, recyclable products
made from wood grown in sustainable forests. The manufacturing processes
conform to the environmental regulations of the country of origin.

*I would like to dedicate this book
to my Mum and Dad and to my brother Paul*

FOREWORD
BY TOMMY SMITH MBE

THE LIVERPOOL FC QUIZ BOOK brings back so many
wonderful memories from my time as a player and I will
never forget walking through the doors of Anfield to sign
schoolboy forms for the legendary Bill Shankly's up-and-
coming team on 19 May 1960. I had just turned 15 and over
the following 18 years I played alongside some truly
wonderful players, all Kop legends in their own right.

And speaking of the Kop, can I just say a special thanks to
every man, woman and child who stood or sat on the
famous terraces cheering on the team throughout the 100
years of its existence. Indeed, my warmest thanks go to
every Liverpool fan out there for your most loyal and
unwavering support down the years.

There is something for every fan in this book. Marc has
just about covered all you would ever want to know about
the club – the history; the leagues; Cup competitions;
European campaigns; players and managers. What I like

most about the book is the way Marc has divided it into 150 separate sections with 10 questions per section. As soon as I opened the book, I was hooked and I know you, too, will have endless hours of fun testing your own knowledge of the Reds, not to mention testing the knowledge of your mates at school, at work, down the local pub or at the game.

I must admit there was the odd question or two that really caught me out... and quite a few I should have known because I played in those games! There were also several that left me scratching my head because I know I should have known the answer but wasn't just 100 per cent certain. I must admit to having enjoyed the odd fierce tackle or two during my playing career, but I have to say that tackling all 1,500 questions in Marc's book was just as enjoyable and definitely not as painful.

So, in closing, I wish Marc luck. It is evident that he has put a lot of commitment, energy and time into compiling this book and I think it is wonderful to see a young man write such a challenging and interesting book that I know all Reds fans out there will want in their book collection. Well done to John Blake Publishing for supporting Marc who, at 18, is just starting out on what will hopefully be a successful career for him as an author.

You'll never walk alone.

TOMMY SMITH MBE, LIVERPOOL 1960–78
638 appearances, 48 goals – 4 First Division Championship winners' medals (1966, 1973, 1976 and 1977); 2 FA Cup winners' medals (1965 and 1974); European Cup winners' medal (1977); 2 UEFA Cup winners' medals (1973 and 1976); European Super Cup winners' medal (1977)

INTRODUCTION

I AM PLEASED to say that this is my third book and I am very grateful to Steve Burdett and Michelle Signore at John Blake Publishing for showing faith in my abilities. My utmost thanks must also go to Tommy Smith, a true Liverpudlian and Liverpool Football Club legend, for agreeing to provide the Foreword to my book.

Liverpool Football Club has a glorious past dating back to the club's formation in 1892 and I would like to think that the 1,500 questions in my book have encapsulated all of the glory years from Liverpool's 18 First DivisionChampionships to their five European Cup wins.

Liverpool Football Club has enjoyed so many successful seasons with so many truly gifted players famously wearing the all-red strip and, of course, some truly iconic managers in charge of the team – Tom Watson, Bill Shankly and Bob Paisley. Within the book, I have covered all 18 First Division Championship wins, the seven FA Cup wins, the seven

League Cup wins, the three UEFA Cup wins, the three UEFA Super Cup wins and, of course, the five European Cup/UEFA Champions League victories. There are also many sections on famous Liverpool players, past and present, and the odd sprinkling of trivia.

I hope you enjoy my book and that you and your friends and family enjoy testing one another on what the team won, where they won it and how it was won in the history of Liverpool Football Club.

Marc White, May 2009

THE QUESTIONS

TROPHIES

1. How many times did Liverpool win the old First Division Championship?

2. The Reds have also won the old Second Division Championship, but how many times?

3. Up to the end of season 2007/08, how many times had the Reds lifted the FA Cup?

4. Liverpool hold the record for most League Cup wins, but how many times have they won this trophy, including the 2008/09 competition?

5. Including the 2008/09 season, how many times have Liverpool won the FA Charity/Community Shield outright?

TROPHIES

6. How many times have the Reds lifted the famous European Cup/UEFA Champions League trophy?

7. Can you recall the number of UEFA Cups the Reds have won?

8. Liverpool have also lifted the European Super Cup, but how many times – 2, 3 or 4?

9. Which one-off trophy did the Reds win in the 1985/86 season?

10. Can you name the Cup competition contested at Anfield by Liverpool and invited opposition which the Reds have won three times?

JOHN ALDRIDGE

1. Prior to signing for Liverpool, which club did John play for?

2. In which year did John sign for the Reds?

3. To the nearest 10, how many League appearances did John make for Liverpool?

4. Can you name the Welsh County where John began his professional football career in 1979?

5. In which year did John leave Liverpool?

6. Name the Spanish club he signed for after leaving Anfield.

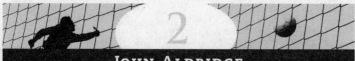

JOHN ALDRIDGE

7. In 1991, which Rovers was John playing for?

8. How many League goals did John score for Liverpool – 40, 50 or 60?

9. Although he was born in England, for which country did John play international football during his career?

10. Against which West Midlands club did John make his League début for Liverpool?

FA CUP 1976/77

1. Which team beat Liverpool in the 1977 FA Cup Final?

2. Who was the Liverpool manager at Wembley in 1977?

3. Can you recall the Reds' goal scorer in the Final?

4. Liverpool needed a replay to dispose of this London club in Round 3. Name them.

5. Who scored for Liverpool in Rounds 3, 4 and 5?

6. Can you recall the team Liverpool beat in the semi-final?

3

FA CUP 1976/77

7. Liverpool disposed of an Athletic side in Round 5 but can you name them?

8. Name the North-East club that lost to Liverpool in the quarter-finals.

9. How many goals did Liverpool score in their 1976/77 FA Cup campaign – 11, 14 or 17?

10. At which ground did Liverpool beat their semi-final opponents?

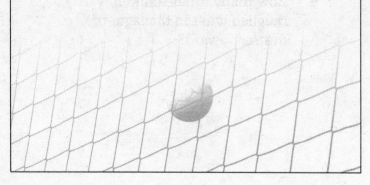

KENNY DALGLISH (I)

1. In which Scottish city was Kenny born?

2. Can you recall the year in which Kenny joined the Reds?

3. How many League appearances did Kenny make for Liverpool – 355, 368 or 386?

4. Which club gave him his first taste of management?

5. Name the Liverpool manager who brought him to Anfield.

6. How many times did Kenny Dalglish win the Manager of the Year award?

KENNY DALGLISH (I)

7. From which club did Liverpool sign Kenny?

8. Can you name the FC Barcelona striker who took Kenny's place in the Scotland squad that travelled to Mexico for the 1986 World Cup Finals after Kenny injured himself in the 1986 FA Cup Final?

9. Against which European country did Kenny score for Scotland in the 1978 World Cup Finals in Argentina?

10. Name either of the English clubs where Kenny had a trial and who subsequently rejected him before he began his professional playing career in Scotland.

INTERNATIONALS (I)

1. Who is the only Liverpool player to have won more than 50 caps for England without ever scoring for his country?

2. Name the first player to be capped by the Netherlands while playing for the Reds.

3. Which country did Istvan Kozma represent at international level?

4. Can you name the former legendary Liverpool captain who scored a total of eight goals for Scotland?

5. This player is the only Chilean international to have played for the Reds. Can you name him?

INTERNATIONALS (I)

6. Which two Reds are the only two players to have played for Liverpool in a World Cup Final?

7. Which international side does Nabib El Zhar represent?

8. Name any one of the four Liverpool players who played in a war-time International for Scotland during their Anfield career.

9. From which Primera Liga club did the Reds sign Alvaro Arbeloa?

10. Can you name the two Israeli internationals that played for Liverpool prior to Yossi Benayoun?

THE MERSEYSIDE DERBY (I)

1. In which year was the inaugural Merseyside derby between Liverpool FC and Everton FC played – 1894, 1896 or 1898?

2. Everton currently hold the longest unbeaten run in matches home and away. To the nearest four, how many games does the unbeaten record stretch to?

3. The longest unbroken winning run at home belongs to Liverpool. How many games does this involve?

4. The record victory in a league match is 6–0 recorded by Liverpool at Goodison Park in the 1930s. In which season during the mid-1930s did this occur?

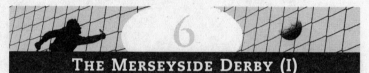

THE MERSEYSIDE DERBY (I)

5. Everton's 2–1 away win in 1995/96 was their first at Anfield in how many years?

6. How many times did Liverpool beat Everton during Joe Royle's two-and-a-half-year reign covering five derby games?

7. Who is the Blues' legend who holds the record for most derby match appearances?

8. How many times have Everton drawn with Liverpool in an FA Cup tie including replays?

9. In which season did Everton last beat Liverpool at Anfield?

10. Everton's 3–0 victory over Liverpool in September 2006 was their biggest League Merseyside derby win for how many years – 32, 42 or 52?

THE PREMIERSHIP YEARS (I)

1. Apart from Liverpool, name any of the remaining 21 inaugural members of the FA Premier League in season 1992/93.

2. Which club beat Liverpool to the Premiership crown in season 2008/09?

3. Can you name Tottenham Hotspur player who won the 1994/95 Football Writers' Player of the Year Award but failed to score against Liverpool?

4. Name the club that finished one place above Liverpool in the Premiership in season 1995/96 and runners-up to Champions Manchester United.

5. Including the 2008/09 season, how many different clubs has Liverpool played in a Premier League match – 39, 41 or 43?

THE PREMIERSHIP YEARS (I)

6. In season 1996/97, Liverpool finished in fourth place in the Premier League. Can you name the former European Cup holders who finished bottom of the table and were relegated?

7. Liverpool is one of only eight English clubs who have never played their football outside the top two Divisions of English football. Can you name five of the remaining seven?

8. Liverpool were the only Premier League club not to have what on display prior to a home game in the Premiership in season 2008/09?

9. Which Midlands club did Liverpool defeat 2–0 away on the opening day of the 2008/09 season?

10. Prior to the start of the 2000/01 season, which Blue became the first Everton player in over 40 years to move across Stanley Park and sign for Liverpool?

HISTORY

1. In which year were Liverpool FC formed?

2. Before it became the home of Liverpool FC, which club played their home matches at Anfield?

3. In which year, in the 1960s, did Liverpool first win the FA Cup?

4. Against which London side did the Reds celebrate 100 years of the Kop at Anfield on 26 August 2006?

5. Liverpool's record attendance of 61,905 was set on 2 February 1952 in an FA Cup fourth-round match. Can you name the opponents they beat 2–1?

HISTORY

6. In which year did Liverpool FC first lift the European Cup?

7. What is the name of the man who founded Liverpool FC?

8. Can you recall the three trophies Liverpool won in 2001, giving them a Cup Treble?

9. Can you name Liverpool's first two 'joint' managers?

10. Which legendary Liverpool manager said, 'Some people believe football is a matter of life and death. I am very disappointed with that attitude. I can assure you it is much, much more important than that'?

9

ALAN KENNEDY

1. In which North-East city was Alan born?

2. At which club did he begin his professional playing career in 1972?

3. In which year did Alan sign for Liverpool?

4. Apart from Liverpool, which other team beat Newcastle United with Alan in the team in a Wembley Cup Final?

5. During the 1976/77 season, Alan scored the only goal of the game for Newcastle United against rivals Middlesbrough at St James' Park. Can you name either of the 'Boro players in the game who would later be his team-mates at Liverpool?

ALAN KENNEDY

6. On his Liverpool début, Alan almost scored an own-goal in Liverpool's 2–1 First Division win at Anfield over which high-flying London club at the time?

7. What was the first major trophy Alan won with Liverpool?

8. What affectionate nickname did the Liverpool fans give Alan?

9. Can you name the Liverpool manager who sold Alan?

10. Which club did Alan join when he left Anfield?

THIS IS ANFIELD

1. In which year was Anfield built – 1884, 1885 or 1886?

2. What is the name of the road which is situated directly behind the Kop grandstand?

3. Prior to its refurbishment and extension in the summer of 1992, what was the name of the Centenary Stand?

4. Liverpool were one of the last Premier League clubs to install an electronic scoreboard. In which year was it installed?

5. Can you name the set of gates through which the players walk after they get off their coach?

6. During the summer of 2000, Liverpool discovered that there was a problem with the upper tier of the Anfield Road Stand that required immediate repair

THIS IS ANFIELD

work for the safety of the fans. What was wrong with the stand?

7. Situated between the corner of the Kop and the Centenary Stand at Anfield stands a flagpole that was formerly a mast on a famous steam ship. Can you name the ship?

8. How many stars has UEFA accredited Anfield with in their 1–5 star stadium rankings?

9. Can you name the South American team England beat 2–1 at Anfield on 1 March 2006 in an international friendly?

10. In November 2007, Liverpool announced plans to leave Anfield and commence the construction of a new stadium in 2008. What name was given to the new stadium when the plans were first unveiled?

PETER BEARDSLEY

1. In which year did Liverpool sign Peter?

2. From which club did Liverpool sign Peter?

3. Can you recall how Peter arrived at the location of the football match in the Carlsberg television advertisement when he played alongside former England internationals in a pub team?

4. Which club did Liverpool sell Peter to?

5. Can you name his former Everton boss who said he was interested in taking charge of the Republic of Ireland national team in 2007 if Peter would work as his assistant?

11

PETER BEARDSLEY

6. How many League goals did he score for Liverpool – 46, 56 or 66?

7. Against which London club did Peter make his League début for the Reds?

8. How much did Liverpool pay for Peter – £0.9m, £1.9m or £2.9m?

9. Can you name the famous North Tyneside Boys Club of which Peter was a product?

10. Which United did Peter play for during the 1982/83 season?

IAN RUSH

1. Prior to signing for the Reds, which club did Ian play for?

2. Ian enjoyed two spells at Liverpool, and between the two he played in Serie A. Which Italian club did he play for?

3. Ian made his début for Liverpool in December 1980 against which team that would go on to win the UEFA Cup that season?

4. During his two spells at Liverpool, Ian made over 400 League appearances for the club, but how many did he make – 469, 489 or 509?

5. In which competition did Ian score his first goal for the Reds on 30 September 1981?

IAN RUSH

6. In which year, in the mid-1990s, did Ian leave the Reds for good?

7. During the 1997/98 season, can you name the club Ian was loaned to?

8. In 2004, Ian was given his chance to manage a football team. Can you recall which one of his former clubs he was appointed the manager of?

9. During the 1998/99 season, which Welsh club did Ian play for?

10. Ian set the record for the most first-team goals scored for Liverpool. How many first-team goals did he score – 346, 366 or 386?

LEAGUE CHAMPIONS 1976/77

1. With how many points did the Reds end the season?

2. The Reds beat which City 1–0 at Anfield on the opening day of the season?

3. Can you name the Midlands club that was the first team to beat the Reds in the League during the season?

4. Name the City which was the last team the Reds beat in a League game in this season.

5. How many of their 21 League home games did Liverpool win?

LEAGUE CHAMPIONS 1976/77

6. Who finished the season as
    the Reds' top League goal
    scorer with 12 goals?

7. On the last day of the League
    season, the Reds lost 2–1 at
    Ashton Gate. Name the City
    they lost to.

8. Can you name the North-East
    club Liverpool beat on New
    Year's Day?

9. Which David scored the Reds'
    last League goal of the season?

10. How many of their last four
    League games did Liverpool
    win on their way to winning
    the First Division
    Championship?

XABI ALONSO

1. What nationality is Xabi?

2. Prior to signing for the Reds, which Spanish club did he play for?

3. Up to the start of the 2008/09 season, what is Xabi's highest career honour?

4. Against which Lancashire club did he make his League début for the Reds?

5. At the beginning of the 2000/01 season, which Spanish club was he loaned to?

XABI ALONSO

6. How much did Liverpool pay for the services of Xabi – £8.5m, £10.5m or £12.5m?

7. In which year did the Reds sign him?

8. Can you name the famous Spanish team Xabi's father, Miguel Ángel Alonso Oyarbide, played for?

9. Can you name the Reds boss who brought Xabi to Anfield?

10. Against which South American country did Xabi make his international début for Spain in April 2003?

INTERNATIONALS (II)

1. Can you name the Red who won more England caps while at Liverpool than any other player who played for the club?

2. Name either of the two Liverpool players who played in a war-time International for England during their Anfield career.

3. This player is the only Swiss international to have played for the Reds.

4. Name the player who has scored more goals for England while with the Reds than any other Liverpool player.

5. Who was the first Brazilian to play for Liverpool?

15

INTERNATIONALS (II)

6.   Name the Red who won more Scotland
     caps during his Liverpool career than
     any other player who played for the
     club.

7.   Can you name the former Liverpool
     player who won more Welsh caps
     during his Anfield career than any
     other player who played for the club?

8.   How many goals did Jason McAteer
     score for the Republic of Ireland during
     his time with Liverpool – 0, 1 or 2?

9.   Which player played for France while
     Liverpool held his registration,
     although he was technically on loan
     away from Anfield at the time he won
     his first international cap?

10. Can you name the only Liverpool
     player to score for Northern Ireland at
     international level?

16

KEVIN KEEGAN

1. Prior to signing for the Reds, which club did Kevin play for?

2. Which London club did Kevin manage during his football career?

3. Can you recall the name of England's opponents when Kevin Keegan took charge of England for the last time as manager?

4. Which team did Kevin play for from 1982 to 1984?

5. After leaving the Reds, can you name the European club for which Kevin signed?

16

KEVIN KEEGAN

6. From 1980 to 1982, which Hampshire-based club did Kevin play for?

7. When he retired from playing, can you name the first club he managed?

8. In which year was Kevin appointed the England manager?

9. Which club did Kevin manage from 2001 to 2005?

10. How many League goals did Kevin score for the Reds – 68, 88 or 108?

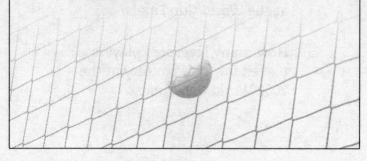

REDS AT THE WORLD CUP (I)

1. The inaugural World Cup Finals took place in Uruguay in 1930. In which year did a Liverpool player first represent his country at the Finals?

2. Name the Liverpool player who Alex Ferguson axed from the Scotland squad that competed in the 1986 World Cup Finals in Argentina.

3. How many Liverpool players played for England at the 2006 World Cup Finals?

4. Who was the first Liverpool goalkeeper to concede a goal at the World Cup Finals?

5. How many Liverpool players played for their country at the 2002 World Cup Finals?

REDS AT THE WORLD CUP (I)

6. Which striker was the first Liverpool player to score a goal for his country at the World Cup Finals?

7. Who was the only Liverpool player to play in the 1994 World Cup Finals in the USA?

8. How many Liverpool players played at least one game at the 1970 World Cup Finals?

9. For which country did the most number of Liverpool players play for their country at the 1982 World Cup Finals in Spain?

10. Which Liverpool player and England international was substituted four times during the 2002 World Cup Finals?

EUROPEAN CHAMPIONSHIP REDS (I)

1. How many Liverpool players played at least one game at the 1960 European Championship Finals?

2. Who was the first Red to play for his country in the European Championship Finals?

3. Which Liverpool player played more games than any other Red at the 1980 European Championship Finals?

4. Who was the first Liverpool goalkeeper to concede a goal at the European Championship Finals?

5. How many Liverpool players scored a goal at the 1988 European Championship Finals?

EUROPEAN CHAMPIONSHIP REDS (I)

6. Which Liverpool player was substituted twice in two of England's three games at the 1988 European Championship Finals?

7. Which Liverpool player played in all five of his country's games at the 1996 European Championship Finals?

8. How many Liverpool players played in the 2000 European Championship Finals?

9. Name any two of the three Liverpool players who played for England in the 2000 European Championship Finals.

10. Name the Liverpool player who was the top goal scorer in the 2004 European Championship Finals.

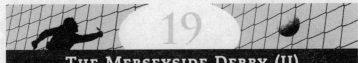

19

THE MERSEYSIDE DERBY (II)

1. When Liverpool won the First Division Championship in season 1963/64, Everton, the reigning Champions, refused to hand over the trophy to be presented to their bitter rivals. What did Liverpool have to celebrate with instead at Anfield?

2. In which season did Liverpool last play Everton four times, excluding replays?

3. Can you name the Everton 'Sandy' who scored an own-goal in the Merseyside derby on 6 December 1969?

4. Can you name the 'Dick' who is the only player to win a First Division Championship winners' medal with Liverpool and Everton?

5. Who was the first Liverpool player sent off in a Premier League Merseyside derby?

THE MERSEYSIDE DERBY (II)

6. Can you name the two players who both scored two goals each after coming on as a substitute in the 1989 Merseyside FA Cup Final?

7. Name the two players who have captained both Everton and Liverpool, although not specifically in a Merseyside derby fixture.

8. Can you name the Everton striker who stopped the Reds' unbeaten run from the start of a season of 29 games in 1988?

9. Up to and including the 2008/09 season, can you name the player who has played in the most number of Premier League Merseyside derby games for Liverpool?

10. Who scored twice for Liverpool in their 2–0 Merseyside derby away win in the Premiership in season 2008/09?

20

MICHAEL OWEN

1. In which year did Michael sign professional terms with Liverpool?

2. How many League appearances did Michael make for Liverpool – 216, 236 or 256?

3. After leaving Anfield, which club did Michael join?

4. In which year did Michael leave Anfield?

5. How old was Michael when he made his League début for Liverpool?

20

MICHAEL OWEN

6. How many League goals did Michael score for Liverpool – 98, 118 or 138?

7. Which club did Michael join when he returned home to England from Spain?

8. Against which team did Michael score a hat-trick in the 1996 FA Youth Cup Final?

9. Which European trophies did Michael win with Liverpool?

10. Can you recall the award Michael received in 2001?

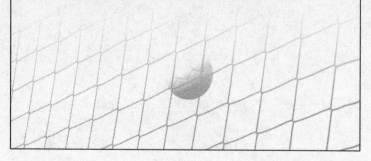

FA CUP WINNERS 1964/65

1. Which team did the Reds beat at Wembley in 1964/65 to lift the FA Cup for the first time?

2. Liverpool beat which Midlands club in Round 3?

3. Who scored for the Reds in three different rounds of the 1964/65 FA Cup?

4. Can you recall the score in the final?

5. Which London club did Liverpool beat in the semi-finals?

FA CUP WINNERS 1964/65

6. Name the manager who guided the Reds to FA Cup glory in 1964/65.

7. Can you recall the City Liverpool disposed of in Round 6?

8. How many of Liverpool's 1964/65 FA Cup ties went to a replay?

9. Can you name the County Liverpool beat in Round 4?

10. Name any Liverpool player who scored in the Final.

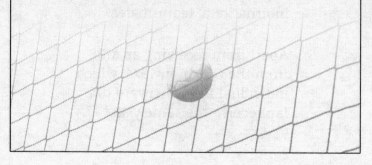

22

IAN CALLAGHAN

1. Can you name the legendary
    Liverpool captain that Ian
    idolised growing up supporting
    Liverpool?

2. Against which Rovers did Ian
    make his Liverpool début on 16
    April 1960 at Anfield?

3. Which was the first trophy Ian
    won with Liverpool?

4. At the end of the 1965/66
    season, Ian joined two Anfield
    team-mates in the England
    squad for the 1966 FIFA World
    Cup Finals to be played in
    England. Name his two
    international team-mates.

5. Apart from receiving an MBE
    from the Queen in 1974, which
    individual football award did
    Ian receive the same year?

22
IAN CALLAGHAN

6. On his Liverpool début, Alan almost scored an own-goal in Liverpool's 2–1 First Division win at Anfield over which high-flying London club at the time?

7. What affectionate nickname did the Liverpool fans give Ian?

8. Ian played in Liverpool's first ever League Cup Final at Wembley Stadium that ended 0–0 before they subsequently lost the replay. Who beat them?

9. Can you name the former Liverpool legend who persuaded Ian to join his team after Ian left Liverpool in the summer of 1978?

10. In season 1981/82, Ian played an FA Cup tie for which club, making him the competition's record holder for most number of appearances with 88?

AWAY DAYS (I)

1. If Liverpool visited Eastlands, which team would they be playing away?

2. If Liverpool visited Walker's Stadium, which team would they be playing away?

3. If Liverpool visited Victoria Park, which United would they be playing away?

4. If Liverpool visited Sincil Bank, which City would they be playing away?

5. If Liverpool visited Stonebridge Road, which double-barrelled team would they be playing away?

AWAY DAYS (I)

6. If Liverpool visited the Stadium of Light, which team would they be playing away?

7. If Liverpool visited Kenilworth Road, which Town would they be playing away?

8. If Liverpool visited Galpharm Stadium, which team would they be playing away?

9. If Liverpool visited Moss Rose, which Town would they be playing away?

10. If Liverpool visited The Shay Stadium, which Town would they be playing away?

THE REDS' FIRST SEASON IN EUROPE

1. In which season did the Reds first participate in one of the three major European competitions?

2. Which one of the three major European competitions at the time was the first one the Reds participated in?

3. Can you name the Icelandic team who were the Reds' first ever opponents in one of the three major European competitions?

4. Name the 'Gordon' who scored the Reds' first ever European competition goal.

5. Which Italian team ended Liverpool's first European campaign?

THE REDS' FIRST SEASON IN EUROPE

6.   Can you recall Liverpool's
     Belgian opponents in Round 2?

7.   How many goals did the Reds
     score in their first European
     campaign – 15, 20 or 25?

8.   Liverpool drew 0–0 home and
     away and 2–2 in a play-off at a
     neutral venue with FC Cologne
     in Round 2, but how was the
     tie awarded to the Reds?

9.   Who scored seven goals in
     Liverpool's inaugural European
     campaign?

10. The Reds won the 1st leg of
     the semi-final 3–1 at Anfield
     but went down 3–0 in the
     return leg. Name any Reds
     player who scored in the semi-
     final.

JAN MØLBY

1. In which Danish city was Jan born?

2. To the nearest 10, how many League appearances did Jan make for the Reds?

3. Prior to signing for Liverpool, which Dutch team did Jan play for?

4. In which year did Jan arrive at Anfield?

5. While at Liverpool, Jan was loaned to which Yorkshire club?

25

JAN MØLBY

6. How many League goals did Jan score for the Reds – 34, 44 or 54?

7. Can you recall the year in which Jan left the Reds?

8. How much did Liverpool pay for the services of Jan – £475,000, £575,000 or £675,000?

9. Jan was also on loan at a Norfolk-based team during his Liverpool career. Name the City concerned.

10. Which team did Jan sign for when he left Anfield?

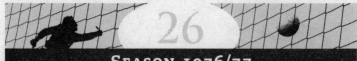

SEASON 1976/77

1. How many games did Liverpool play at Anfield in their 1976/77 FA Cup campaign?

2. Which winger scored Liverpool's first League goal of the 1976/77 season?

3. Name either of the two Liverpool scorers in their first round, first-leg European Cup tie.

4. Which team did Liverpool beat in the 1976 FA Charity Shield?

5. Who played their last ever game for Liverpool in the 1977 FA Cup Final?

SEASON 1976/77

6. Can you recall the 1966 World Cup winner who brought his 'XI' team to Anfield on 27 May 1977 for Tommy Smith's Testimonial?

7. Which Midlands club put Liverpool out of the 1976/77 League Cup?

8. Who scored two penalties for Liverpool during their 1976/77 FA Cup campaign?

9. Apart from Kevin Keegan, name the other Red who scored four times in Liverpool's 1976/77 FA Cup campaign.

10. How many games did the Reds play in the 1976/77 European Cup?

THE SPORTING YEAR (I)

1. In which year did Peter Thompson arrive at Liverpool from Preston North End for £30,000, Ayala win the Grand National, Chuck McKinley (USA) win the Wimbledon Men's Singles Championship, Yorkshire win the County Championship and Manchester United win the FA Cup?

2. In which year did Liverpool win the League Cup, Royal Athlete win the Grand National, Pete Sampras (USA) win the Wimbledon Men's Singles Championship, Warwickshire win the County Championship and Blackburn Rovers win the Premier League?

27

THE SPORTING YEAR (I)

3. In which year did Liverpool finish runners-up to Everton in the First Division, Steve Davis win the World Professional Snooker Championship, John Lowe win the BDO World Darts Championship and Coventry City win the FA Cup?

4. In which year did Liverpool win the European Cup, Red Rum win the Grand National, Virginia Wade win the Wimbledon Ladies' Singles Championship, Kent and Middlesex share the County Championship and Manchester United win the FA Cup?

5. In which year did Liverpool win the FA Cup, Jay Trump win the Grand National, Roy Emerson (Australia) win the Wimbledon Men's Singles

THE SPORTING YEAR (I)

Championship, Worcestershire won the County Championship and Manchester United win the First Division Championship?

6. In which year did Bill Shankly sign Phil Boersma and Alun Evans, Red Alligator win the Grand National, Billie Jean King (USA) win the Wimbledon Ladies' Singles Championship, Yorkshire win the County Championship and Manchester United win the European Cup?

7. In which year did John Toshack arrive at Liverpool from Cardiff City, Ray Reardon win the World Professional Snooker Championship, Feyenoord win the European Cup and Chelsea win the FA Cup?

27

THE SPORTING YEAR (I)

8. In which year did Bob Paisley retire from playing, Jaroslav Drobny (Egypt) win the Wimbledon Men's Championship, Surrey win the County Championship, Wolverhampton Wanderers win the First Division Championship and West Bromwich Albion win the FA Cup?

9. In which year did Liverpool become First Division Champions, Gay Trip win the Grand National, Boris Becker (Germany) win the Wimbledon Men's Singles Championship and Essex win the County Championship?

10. In which year did Liverpool win the First Division Championship and League Cup, Hallo Dandy win the Grand National, Joe Johnson win the World Professional Snooker Championship and Eric Bristow win the BDO World Darts Championship?

LANDMARK PREMIERSHIP GOALS

1. Can you name the winger who scored Liverpool's first ever goal in the FA Premier League in a game against Sheffield United at Anfield on 19 August 1992?

2. Who scored the Reds' 750th Premiership goal on 4 April 2004 against Blackburn Rovers at Anfield?

3. Michael Owen scored the Reds' 500th Premiership goal in a game at Highfield Road. Who were the opponents?

4. Can you name the United against whom Nigel Clough scored Liverpol's 100th Premiership goal in a game at Anfield on 4 January 1994?

5. Who scored the Reds' 100th Premiership goal in a 2–2 draw

LANDMARK PREMIERSHIP GOALS

with Manchester United at Old Trafford on 1 October 1995?

6. Which striker scored the Reds' 250th (1996) and 300th Premiership goal (1997)?

7. The Reds scored their 750th FA Premier League goal against which team that won the Premiership in 1994/95?

8. Michael Owen scored the Reds' 700th Premiership goal in a game at the Hawthorns. Who were the opponents?

9. Which non-British midfielder scored Liverpool's 650th Premiership goal against his former team?

10. Liverpool's 350th Premiership goal was scored against their 1974 FA Charity Shield opponents. Name them.

THE MERSEYSIDE DERBY (III)

1. Can you name the Everton striker who, when he scored a goal against Liverpool at Anfield, would turn to the Kop and bow gracefully in a posture like a matador?

2. The longest unbroken winning run away from home in Merseyside derbies belongs to Everton. How many games does this involve – 7, 9 or 11?

3. To the nearest 5,000, what is the largest crowd ever to watch a Merseyside derby game at Everton which is also Everton's largest attendance in the club's history?

4. In which year during the late 1940s did the above Merseyside derby take place?

5. What did Liverpool and Everton fans link together from Goodison Park to Anfield in remembrance of the 96 Liverpool fans who died at Hillsborough in April 1989?

29

THE MERSEYSIDE DERBY (III)

6. In the 1990/91 FA Cup, the two sides played out an exhilarating 4–4 draw at Goodison Park in a fifth-round replay. How many times were Liverpool in front in the game before Everton fought back to force a second replay?

7. Following on from the Merseyside derby FA Cup 4–4 draw in 1990/91, what happened later in the week?

8. Liverpool holds the longest unbeaten run in Merseyside derby home matches. How many games does this extend to – 14, 17 or 20?

9. The longest unbeaten run away from home is held by Everton. How many games does this extend to – 15, 18 or 21?

10. How many of the 11 Merseyside derbies played between the autumns of 1994 and 1999 did Liverpool win?

EUROPEAN CUP WINNERS 1976/77

1. Which team did Liverpool beat in the 1977 European Cup Final?

2. The Reds met Northern Ireland opposition in the first round. Can you recall their opponents?

3. Which city hosted the 1977 European Cup Final?

4. Can you recall the Reds' highest aggregate win in the 1976/77 competition?

5. Name the Swiss side the Reds disposed of in the semi-finals.

6. Can you recall the French side Liverpool beat en route to lifting the European Cup in 1977?

7. Liverpool beat Trabzonspor
    over two legs in the second
    round. Which country are they
    from?

8. Name any player who scored
    for the Reds in the Final.

9. Which player scored Liverpool's
    third goal in a 3–1 win in their
    second-leg quarter-final tie
    which guaranteed their place
    in the semi-finals?

10. Name either of the Liverpool
    players who each scored four
    goals in the Reds' successful
    1976/77 European Cup
    campaign.

PREMIER OWN-GOALS AND HOWLERS

1. Andy Barlow was the first player to score an own-goal in the Premier League against the Reds. Which Athletic team was he playing for?

2. Which Scottish international was the first Liverpool player to score an own-goal in the Premier League?

3. Can you name the not-so-sharp centre-half who was the first Liverpool player to score an own-goal in the Premier League at Anfield?

4. Name the future Red who scored an own-goal for Liverpool against Coventry City on 14 March 1995 at Anfield.

5. Which Claus was the first player to score an own-goal in the Premier League against the Reds in a Merseyside derby?

PREMIER OWN-GOALS AND HOWLERS

6. Can you name the England centre-half who scored an own-goal in the Premier League against Liverpool at Elland Road on 3 February 2002?

7. Name the unfortunate Red who scored two own-goals against Manchester United at Anfield on 11 September 1999.

8. Who, on 1 October 2000, was the first Liverpool goalkeeper to score an own-goal in the Premier League?

9. Name the Wimbledon defender, and future Red, who scored an own-goal at Anfield on 28 December 1993.

10. Which Reds centre-half was the first Liverpool player to score an own-goal in the Premier League in a Merseyside derby?

EUROPEAN CUP WINNERS 1983/84

1. Which team did Liverpool beat in the 1984 European Cup Final?

2. The Reds played which Danish club in the first round?

3. Which city hosted the 1984 European Cup Final?

4. Can you recall the Reds' highest aggregate win in the 1983/84 competition?

5. Name the Romanian side the Reds beat in the semi-finals.

6. Can you recall the Portuguese side Liverpool beat en route to lifting the European Cup in 1984?

32

EUROPEAN CUP WINNERS 1983/84

7. Liverpool met Spanish opposition in the second round. Can you recall which team they played?

8. Name the only player who scored for the Reds before extra-time in the Final.

9. To the nearest 10,000, what was the attendance at the Final?

10. Who was Liverpool's top goal scorer in the 1983/84 European Cup and how many goals did he score?

33

TERRY McDERMOTT

1. Prior to signing for Liverpool, which club did Terry play for?

2. In which year did Terry sign for the Reds?

3. To the nearest 10, how many League appearances did Terry make for Liverpool?

4. After leaving Anfield, which team did Terry sign for?

5. Can you recall the name of the Irish team Terry played for in 1984?

33

TERRY McDERMOTT

6. Terry played for a Greek team in 1985 but can you name them?

7. At which Lancashire club did Terry begin his professional career?

8. How many League goals did Terry score for the Reds – 44, 54 or 64?

9. Can you recall the year in which Terry left Anfield?

10. Which club gave Terry a coaching job in 2005?

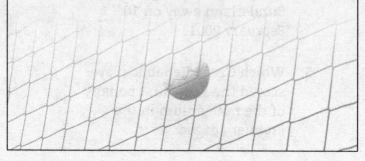

PREMIER SPOT-KICK SCORERS

1. Which midfielder scored the Reds' first penalty in the Premier League?

2. Which winger scored three consecutive penalties in the Premier League for Liverpool between 17 April 1993 and 8 May 1993?

3. Against which London team, First Division Champions in 1961, did Robbie Fowler score a penalty for the Reds on 18 December 1993?

4. Which Finnish international scored a penalty against Sunderland away on 10 February 2001?

5. Which Czech Republic player scored the Reds' first penalty of the millennium in the Premier League?

34

PREMIER SPOT-KICK SCORERS

6. Against which London team did Milan Baros score two penalties for the Reds on 13 November 2004 at Anfield?

7. Can you name the England international who scored the Reds' last goal in the Premier League before the millennium?

8. This Scottish international scored a penalty against Tottenham Hotspur on 22 April 2001. Can you name him?

9. Who scored his first Premiership penalty for Liverpool against Wimbledon away on 9 August 1997?

10. Apart from Michael Owen, who else scored a penalty for the Reds in a Premier League match in season 2002/03?

ELISHA SCOTT

1. In which position did Elisha play for the Reds?

2. Prior to signing for Liverpool, which very famous Northern Ireland-based club did Elisha play for?

3. To the nearest 50, how many League appearances did Elisha make for the Reds?

4. Name the two international teams Elisha played for during his career.

5. How many international caps did Elisha win during his time at Anfield – 17, 27 or 37?

35

ELISHA SCOTT

6. In which year during the 1910s did the Reds sign Elisha?

7. Elisha played for a Northern Ireland-based club when he was just 14 years old. Can you name the team whose home is also the home venue for Northern Ireland international matches?

8. In which year during the early 1930s did Elisha leave Anfield?

9. Can you recall the American-sounding United which Elisha played for during his career?

10. Elisha was offered a job at Belfast Celtic in 1934. What position was he offered?

THE EUROPEAN CUP

1. Can you name the Gerry who scored the Reds' first ever European Cup goal at Anfield?

2. What was so unusual about the Reds' 100th goal in the European Cup?

3. Prior to the creation of the UEFA Champions League, who was the last team Liverpool played in the European Cup?

4. Prior to the creation of the UEFA Champions League, who was the last Liverpool player to score a goal in the European Cup?

5. Who scored the Reds' 100th goal in the European Cup against Oulun Palloseura on 30 September 1981?

36

THE EUROPEAN CUP

6. How many times did Liverpool win the 'old' European Cup (prior to the creation of the UEFA Champions League)?

7. In which year were the Reds first crowned Champions of Europe?

8. Which striker scored the Reds' 50th away goal in the European Cup versus Dinamo Bucharest on 25 April 1984?

9. How many European Cup campaigns did the Reds participate in (prior to the creation of the UEFA Champions League)?

10. To the nearest 10, how many goals did the Reds score in the European Cup (prior to the creation of the UEFA Champions League)?

JOHN BARNES

1. In which Caribbean country was John born?

2. Can you recall the year in which Liverpool signed John?

3. Prior to signing for the Reds, which club did he play for?

4. To the nearest 10, how many League appearances did John make during his Anfield career?

5. After leaving Anfield, which team did John sign for?

6. Name the London club where John ended his playing career in 1999.

37

JOHN BARNES

7. How many League goals did he score for Liverpool – 84, 94 or 104?

8. For which Scottish club was John Barnes a player-manager in season 1999/2000, although he never actually made any appearances for them?

9. Against which London club did John make his League début for the Reds?

10. Which team was John appointed the manager of in September 2008?

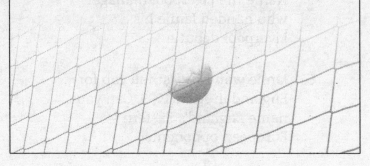

38

JAMIE CARRAGHER

1. What did Jamie win with Liverpool in 1996?

2. Can you name the competition in which Carra made his senior début for Liverpool on 8 January 1997?

3. Name the North-East club against which Jamie made his senior début.

4. Carra marked his Premiership début for the Reds with a goal. Who were Liverpool's Midlands opponents?

5. Name the Liverpool manager who handed Jamie his Liverpool début.

6. Jamie won his first full cap for England in April 1999. Can you name England's Eastern European opponents?

38

JAMIE CARRAGHER

7. Can you name the Blackburn Rovers player whose forceful tackle on Jamie at Ewood Park forced him to miss six months of the 2003/04 season?

8. In November 2006, whose club record of 89 European appearances did Carra break?

9. Against which club did Jamie make his 500th appearance for the Reds in an FA Cup tie at Anfield on 15 January 2008?

10. In season 2007/08, Carra played his 100th European game for the Reds. Can you name the Italian Serie A side who provided the opposition and who Liverpool dumped out of the competition?

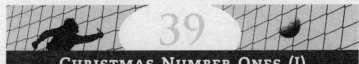

CHRISTMAS NUMBER ONES (I)

1. Liverpool finished in 4th place in the FA Premier League in 1995 and Michael Jackson had the UK Christmas Number One. Can you recall the name of the song?

2. Liverpool finished in 2nd place in the FA Premier League in 2002. Which group had the UK Christmas Number One hit that year with 'Sorry Seems to Be the Hardest Word'?

3. Liverpool finished in 5th place in the FA Premier League when Kelly and Ozzy Osbourne had the UK Christmas Number One the same year with 'Changes'. What was the year?

4. Liverpool won Division 1 in 1986 and the Housemartins had the UK Christmas Number One. Can you recall the name of the song?

CHRISTMAS NUMBER ONES (I)

5. Liverpool finished in 2nd place in Division 1 and Queen had the UK Christmas Number One the same year with 'Bohemian Rhapsody/These Are the Days of Our Lives'. What was the year?

6. Liverpool finished in 7th place in the FA Premier League in 1999. Which group had the UK Christmas Number One hit that year with 'I Have a Dream/Seasons in the Sun'?

7. Liverpool won Division 1 and Pink Floyd had the UK Christmas Number One the same year with 'Another Brick in the Wall'. What was the year?

8. Liverpool finished 5th in Division 1 in 1971 and Benny Hill had the UK Christmas Number One. Can you recall the name of the song?

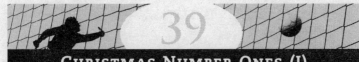

CHRISTMAS NUMBER ONES (I)

9. Liverpool finished in 3rd place in Division 1 in 1972. Who had the UK Christmas Number One hit that year with 'Long-Haired Lover from Liverpool'?

10. Liverpool finished 5th in Division 1 and Dave Edmunds had the UK Christmas Number One the same year with 'I Hear You Knocking'. What was the year?

40

NICKNAMES (I)

Match the player with
his nickname:

1.	Robbie Fowler	*Crazy Horse*
2.	Steve McManaman	*Mighty Mouse*
3.	Neil Ruddock	*Digger*
4.	Emlyn Hughes	*Big Bamber*
5.	Ron Yeats	*God*
6.	Kevin Keegan	*Nando*
7.	Steve Heighway	*Anfield Iron*
8.	John Barnes	*Rowdy*
9.	Fernando Morientes	*Shaggy*
10.	Tommy Smith	*Razor*

INTERNATIONALS (III)

1. Name the Red who won more Northern Ireland caps during his entire career than any other player who played for the club.

2. Can you name the only Swedish international to play for Liverpool?

3. Which country did Jari Litmanen represent at international level?

4. Who was the first Liverpool player capped by Portugal?

5. Up to the end of the 2008/09 season, name the only Croatian international to have played for the Reds.

INTERNATIONALS (III)

6. Can you name the first Slovakian international to play for Liverpool?

7. Name the David who won three caps for Northern Ireland as a Liverpool player.

8. Name the Liverpool player who, during his Anfield career, scored 26 times for England at full international level.

9. Can you name the two German internationals who played for Liverpool in season 2000/01?

10. Up to the end of the 2008/09 season, name the only USA international to play for the Reds.

FORMER AWAY GROUNDS

1. If Liverpool had paid a visit to Maine Road in the past, which team would have been the home side?

2. If Liverpool had paid a visit to Filbert Street in the past, which team would have been the home side?

3. If Liverpool had paid a visit to Burnden Park in the past, which team would have been the home side?

4. If Liverpool had paid a visit to Ayresome Park in the past, which team would have been the home side?

5. If Liverpool had paid a visit to Plough Lane in the past, which team would have been the home side?

FORMER AWAY GROUNDS

6. If Liverpool had paid a visit to The Goldstone Ground in the past, which team would have been the home side?

7. If Liverpool had paid a visit to Highfield Road in the past, which team would have been the home side?

8. If Liverpool had paid a visit to The Dell in the past, which team would have been the home side?

9. If Liverpool had paid a visit to Elm Park in the past, which team would have been the home side?

10. If Liverpool had paid a visit to The Baseball Ground in the past, which team would have been the home side?

FERNANDO TORRES

1. In which Spanish city was Fernando born – Barcelona, Madrid or Valencia?

2. Which sportswear-sponsored Cup was the first competition Fernando won?

3. Can you name the club Fernando turned down the chance of joining after the 2006 World Cup Finals?

4. From which Spanish club did Liverpool purchase Fernando?

5. Against which country did he make his début for Spain on 6 September 2003 – England, France or Portugal?

FERNANDO TORRES

6. Against which Midlands club did Fernando make his competitive début for Liverpool?

7. Name the London team he scored his first Premier League goal against which marked his Anfield début.

8. In which competition did Fernando score his first hat-trick for Liverpool?

9. Can you recall the name of the Portuguese side against which he scored his first UEFA Champions League goal for the Reds?

10. Name the country against which Fernando scored the winning goal of the game for Spain in the 2008 European Championships Final.

THE MERSEYSIDE DERBY (IV)

1. Which striker was the first player to score for both Everton and Liverpool in a Merseyside derby?

2. Following on from Question 1, name the only other player to score for both Everton and Liverpool in a Merseyside derby.

3. Can you name either of the Liverpool players who were sent off in the Premier League Merseyside derby at Anfield on 27 September 1999?

4. The last penalty scored in a Merseyside derby came in the 2007/08 season. Who scored it?

5. What did Everton manage in season 1888/89 that they had never done before against Liverpool?

THE MERSEYSIDE DERBY (IV)

6. This striker has scored more
    Premier League goals against
    Liverpool in a Merseyside derby
    than any other player. Who is he?

7. In which season did Everton last
    beat Liverpool in the two
    Merseyside derby League
    games?

8. Three Everton players have
    scored a penalty in a Merseyside
    derby for the Toffees. Name any
    one of the three.

9. Who has scored the most
    number of Premier League goals
    for Liverpool in Merseyside
    derbies?

10. Prior to the 2008/09 season, in
    which season did the Reds last
    meet the Toffees in the FA Cup?

WHO ARE WE PLAYING? (I)

1. If Liverpool were in opposition against the Gunners, who would they be playing?

2. If Liverpool were in opposition against the Seagulls, who would they be playing?

3. If Liverpool were in opposition against the Tykes, who would they be playing?

4. If Liverpool were in opposition against the Bees, name either of the teams that they could be playing.

5. If Liverpool were in opposition against the Stanley, who would they be playing?

WHO ARE WE PLAYING? (I)

6. If Liverpool were in opposition against the Villains, who would they be playing?

7. If Liverpool were in opposition against the Clarets, who would they be playing?

8. If Liverpool were in opposition against the Tangerines, who would they be playing?

9. If Liverpool were in opposition against the Pirates, who would they be playing?

10. If Liverpool were in opposition against the Brewers, which Albion would they be playing?

LEAGUE CHAMPIONS 1983/84

1. To the nearest 10, how many points did the Reds end the season with?

2. Can you name the Wanderers the Reds drew 1–1 away with on the opening day of the season?

3. Can you name the Lancashire club that was the first team to beat the Reds in the League during the season?

4. Can you name the North-East club that was the first team to beat Liverpool at Anfield in this season?

5. How many of their 21 League home games did Liverpool lose?

LEAGUE CHAMPIONS 1983/84

6. Who finished the season as the Reds' top League goal scorer with 32 goals?

7. On the last day of the League season, the Reds drew 1–1 at Anfield. Name the City they drew with.

8. Can you name the Midlands club Liverpool beat on Boxing Day 1983?

9. Which Ian scored the Reds' last League goal of the season?

10. How many of their last four League games did Liverpool win on their way to clinching the First Division Championship?

PLAYERS (I)

1. In 2003, which managerial assistant's job was Stig Inge Bjørnebye given?

2. Which unfortunate Red scored an own-goal on 5 December 1998 and 1 May 1999 in matches against Tottenham Hotspur?

3. Can you name the 'Phil' whom Bill Shankly signed for Liverpool in 1968?

4. Which United did Ian Rush play for in the 1997/98 season?

5. Who scored Liverpool's winner in the 1976 FA Charity Shield?

6. During the 2005/06 season, Steve Staunton was a player/assistant manager at which West Midlands club?

PLAYERS (I)

7. Which former Glasgow Rangers player scored the Reds' 800th Premiership goal on 17 April 1993 against Coventry City at Anfield?

8. Who scored two penalties for Liverpool in Tommy Smith's Testimonial at Anfield in May 1977?

9. Against which London club did Gary Ablett make his début for the Reds?

10. Which future Liverpool player scored a penalty against the Reds in the final League game of the 1992/93 season but it wasn't enough to keep his team in the FA Premier League?

CHRISTMAS NUMBER ONES (II)

1. Liverpool finished in 2nd place in Division 1 in 1974 and Mud had the UK Christmas Number One. Can you recall the name of the song?

2. Liverpool won Division 1 in 1984. Which group had the UK Christmas Number One hit that year with 'Do They Know It's Christmas'?

3. In which year did Liverpool finish in 4th place in the FA Premier League and Bob the Builder had the UK Christmas Number One with 'Can We Fix It?'?

4. Liverpool were Division 1 Champions in 1977 and Wings had the UK Christmas Number One. Can you recall the name of the song?

5. Liverpool finished in 5th place in Division 1 in 1981. Which group had the UK Christmas Number One hit that year with 'Don't You Want Me?'?

CHRISTMAS NUMBER ONES (II)

6. In which year did Liverpool finish in 4th place in the FA Premier League and the Teletubbies had the UK Christmas Number One with 'Teletubbies Say Eh-Oh!'?

7. Liverpool finished in 4th place in the FA Premier League in 2004 and Band Aid 20 had the UK Christmas Number One. Can you recall the name of the song?

8. Liverpool were Division 1 Champions in 1990. Which artist had the UK Christmas Number One hit that year with 'Saviour's Day'?

9. In which year were Liverpool Division 1 Champions and Renee & Renato had the UK Christmas Number One with 'Save Your Love'?

10. Liverpool were Division 1 Champions in 1983 and The Flying Pickets had the UK Christmas Number One. Can you recall the name of the song?

RONNIE WHELAN

1. In which Irish city was Ronnie born?

2. Can you name the Liverpool manager who signed Ronnie for the club?

3. On 3 April 1981, Ronnie made his début for the Reds and scored against which City in a 3–0 First Division win at Anfield?

4. Can you name the famous Liverpool Number 5 whose shirt Ronnie took over on the left side of the Liverpool midfield during the 1981/82 season, bringing the former holder of the shirt's Anfield career to an end in the process?

5. Which was the first major trophy Ronnie won with Liverpool?

RONNIE WHELAN

6. How many First Division League Championship winners' medals did Ronnie win with Liverpool?

7. In season 1988/89, Ronnie was made the captain of Liverpool for much of the season following injury to the club captain. Who was the injured club captain?

8. Which was the last major trophy Ronnie won with Liverpool?

9. Despite scoring in the semi-final against this team, Ronnie missed the Final through injury. Which Final did he miss in season 1991/92?

10. Can you name the United which appointed Ronnie as their player-manager when he left Anfield?

DOMESTIC CUPS 1983/84

1. Which London club did Liverpool beat 8–1 on aggregate in the first round of the League Cup?

2. Can you name the London club Liverpool played three times in the League Cup in the third round, eventually beating them 1–0?

3. Which Midlands club did Liverpool beat 3–0 in the fourth round of the League Cup?

4. In the fifth round of the League Cup, Liverpool played a Yorkshire club and beat them 3–0. Can you name them?

5. Which Midlands club did Liverpool beat 4–1 on aggregate in the semi-finals of the League Cup?

DOMESTIC CUPS 1983/84

6. In the League Cup Final, Liverpool met Lancashire opposition and beat them 1–0. Can you name the club?

7. Who scored Liverpool's first goal of the League Cup campaign?

8. Who scored Liverpool's last goal of the 1983/84 League Cup?

9. Which United did Liverpool beat 4–0 in the third round of the FA Cup?

10. Liverpool were knocked out in the fourth round of the FA Cup. Which Albion beat them 2–0?

INTERNATIONALS (IV)

1. Name the only Liverpool player to play for his country in the 1998 Gold Cup.

2. Name the only Liverpool player to both play for and score for his country in the Final of the African Cup of Nations.

3. How many Liverpool players missed for England in the penalty shoot-out defeat to Portugal at the 2006 World Cup Finals?

4. Which job was Steve Staunton handed on 13 January 2006?

5. How many Liverpool players played at least one game at the 1974 World Cup Finals?

51

INTERNATIONALS (IV)

6. Name any Liverpool player
   who played for their country in
   the 1986 World Cup Finals.

7. This Liverpool player scored
   more goals for his country
   than any other Red at the 2006
   World Cup Finals in Germany.
   Can you name him?

8. Apart from Liverpool's England
   players, name any other Red
   who scored for a European
   side at the 2006 World Cup
   Finals in Germany.

9. Name the only Liverpool player
   to play for his country in the
   2000 Gold Cup.

10. Who was the only Liverpool
    player to score for his country
    at the 1982 World Cup Finals in
    Spain?

WHO ARE WE PLAYING? (II)

1. If Liverpool were in opposition against the Trotters, who would they be playing?

2. If Liverpool were in opposition against the Bluebirds, who would they be playing?

3. If Liverpool were in opposition against the Cherries, who would they be playing?

4. If Liverpool were in opposition against the Cumbrians, who would they be playing?

5. If Liverpool were in opposition against the Shots, what Town would they be playing?

52

WHO ARE WE PLAYING? (II)

6. If Liverpool were in opposition against the Addicks, who would they be playing?

7. If Liverpool were in opposition against the Sky Blues, who would they be playing?

8. If Liverpool were in opposition against the Bantams, who would they be playing?

9. If Liverpool were in opposition against the Exiles, who would they be playing?

10. If Liverpool were in opposition against the Yellows, who would they be playing?

AWAY DAYS (II)

1. If Liverpool visited the Reebok Stadium, which team would they be playing away?

2. If Liverpool visited Gresty Road, which team would they be playing away?

3. If Liverpool visited Griffin Park, which team would they be playing away?

4. If Liverpool visited Brunton Park, which United would they be playing away?

5. If Liverpool visited Valley Parade, which City would they be playing away?

53

AWAY DAYS (II)

6. If Liverpool visited the Valley, which team would they be playing away?

7. If Liverpool visited Selhurst Park, which team would they be playing away?

8. If Liverpool visited Ashton Gate, which team would they be playing away?

9. If Liverpool visited Whaddon Park, which Town would they be playing away?

10. If Liverpool visited Park Lane, which team would they be playing away?

54

SHIRT SPONSORS

1. Which sponsorship logo, not shirt manufacturer, appeared on the Liverpool home shirt in season 1987/88?

2. Which company sponsored the English First Division when Liverpool played in it in season 1980/81?

3. Which sports company manufactured the Liverpool kit in season 1980/81?

4. Which sponsorship logo, not shirt manufacturer, appeared on the Liverpool home shirt in season 1979/80?

5. Which drinks company sponsored the FA Premier League when Liverpool played in it in season 1996/97?

SHIRT SPONSORS

6. Can you name the bank that sponsored the FA Premier League in season 2005/06?

7. Which sponsorship logo, not shirt manufacturer, appeared on the Liverpool home shirt in season 1999/2000?

8. Which sports company manufactured the Liverpool kit in season 2002/03?

9. Which sponsorship logo, not shirt manufacturer, appeared on the Liverpool home shirt in season 1991/92?

10. Which sports company manufactured the Liverpool kit in season 1988/89?

REDS AT THE WORLD CUP (II)

1. Which Laurie was the first Liverpool player to play for England in the World Cup Finals?

2. Name the two Liverpool players who played in the 1978 World Cup Finals in Argentina.

3. Can you name any three Liverpool players who played for their country at the 2002 World Cup Finals?

4. Who was the only Liverpool player to play for England at the 1958 World Cup Finals?

5. Apart from Roger Hunt, which other Red played for England in the 1966 World Cup Finals?

REDS AT THE WORLD CUP (II)

6. Which Liverpool centre-half played for his country at the 1982 World Cup Finals in Spain?

7. Can you name two of the three Liverpool players who played for England in the 1998 World Cup Finals?

8. How many different countries were represented by Liverpool players at the 2006 World Cup Finals?

9. Name any non-British Liverpool player who scored for their country in the 2006 World Cup Finals.

10. Which Red was the only player to score a goal in the 1990 World Cup Finals in Italy, doing so in a penalty shoot-out for his country?

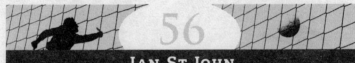

56

IAN ST JOHN

1. In which Scottish town was Ian born?

2. How many League appearances did Ian make for the Reds – 336, 346 or 356?

3. After leaving Liverpool, which City did Ian sign for?

4. Against which Lancashire club did Ian make his League début for Liverpool?

5. How many goals did Ian score on his Reds début?

6. Prior to signing for Liverpool, which Scottish club did Ian play for?

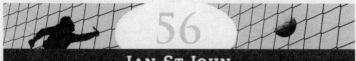

IAN ST JOHN

7. How many League goals did Ian score for the Reds – 85, 90 or 95?

8. In which year did Liverpool sign Ian St John?

9. How many international appearances did Ian make for Scotland?

10. Ian and another ex-footballer hosted a very popular football TV show during the 1980s. Can you name his co-host?

CHAMPIONS OF EUROPE 2004/05

1. What Austrian team did Liverpool beat 2–1 on aggregate in a qualifying game for the competition?

2. In the first and fifth matches of the group stage, Liverpool met which club whose stadium had played host to the European Super Cup Final since 1998?

3. Liverpool played a Greek team in the second and sixth matches of the group stage and the aggregate score was 3–2 to Liverpool. Who were the Reds' opponents?

4. In the third and fourth matches of the group stage, what 'Real' team did the Reds meet?

CHAMPIONS OF EUROPE 2004/05

5. Which German club did Liverpool beat 6–2 on aggregate in the second round of the competition?

6. Liverpool played which team in the quarter-finals of the competition that they had previously met in the Final of the European Cup?

7. Who did the Reds beat in the semi-finals to get to the Final?

8. With which Italian team did Liverpool draw 3–3 after extra-time in the Final?

9. What was the score in the Final's penalty shoot-out?

10. Can you name the Red who scored Liverpool's first goal of the 2004/05 competition?

MIXED BAG (I)

1. Which team did Liverpool both beat and lose to in May 1977?

2. Which foreign striker scored the Reds' 50th Premiership goal on 5 February 2005 against Fulham at Anfield?

3. Which Spanish Red scored an own-goal in a match against Birmingham City at Anfield on 1 February 2006?

4. Can you name the former West Ham United player who scored his first penalty for the Reds against Southampton away on 14 February 1994?

5. Which Premier League club that Liverpool played in season 2008/09 did not have a shirt sponsor for the whole season?

MIXED BAG (I)

6. Tommy Smith's Testimonial in 1977 ended in a very high-scoring draw. What was the final score of the game?

7. If Liverpool had paid a visit to Roker Park in the past, which team would have been the home side?

8. In which year during the early 1980s did Gary Ablett sign for Liverpool?

9. Prior to a match in which the Republic of Ireland were to play the Netherlands, what happened to Steve Staunton?

10. What was so unusual about Liverpool's Round 3 FA Cup tie and the Final in the 1964/65 competition?

WHO ARE WE PLAYING? (III)

1. If Liverpool were in opposition against the Black Cats, who would they be playing?

2. If Liverpool were in opposition against the Railwaymen, who would they be playing?

3. If Liverpool were in opposition against the Robins, which City would they be playing?

4. If Liverpool were in opposition against the Mariners, who would they be playing?

5. If Liverpool were in opposition against the Yellow Army, who would they be playing?

WHO ARE WE PLAYING? (III)

6. If Liverpool were in opposition against the Cottagers, who would they be playing?

7. If Liverpool were in opposition against the Citizens, which City would they be playing?

8. If Liverpool were in opposition against the 'U's, name either of the Uniteds that they could be playing.

9. If Liverpool were in opposition against the Stags, which Town would they be playing?

10. If Liverpool were in opposition against the Daggers, who would they be playing?

EUROPEAN CHAMPIONSHIP REDS (II)

1. How many Liverpool players played at least one game at the 1976 European Championship Finals?

2. How many Liverpool players played for England in the 1980 European Championship Finals?

3. Name any three Liverpool players who played for England in the 1980 European Championship Finals.

4. Who was the first Liverpool player to score a goal at the European Championship Finals?

5. Which Red played in all three of England's games at the 1988 European Championship Finals?

EUROPEAN CHAMPIONSHIP REDS (II)

6. Name any two Liverpool players who played in the 1996 European Championship Finals.

7. How many goals did Fernando Torres score for Spain at the 2008 European Championship Finals?

8. Name the two Liverpool players who played for Norway in the 2000 European Championship Finals.

9. How many Liverpool players played in the 2004 European Championship Finals?

10. Can you name Liverpool's two Czech Republic players who played in the 2000 European Championship Finals?

61

NICKNAMES (II)

Match the player with his
nickname:

1.	David Johnson	*King Kenny*
2.	Tommy Lawrence	*Stan the Man*
3.	Harry Chambers	*Little Bamber*
4.	Rob Jones	*Dave*
5.	Brian Hall Little	*The Flying Pig*
6.	Jason McAteer	*The Wizard of Oz*
7.	Harry Kewell	*Doc*
8.	Paul Ince	*Trigger*
9.	Stan Collymore	*Smiler*
10.	Kenny Dalglish	*The Guv'nor*

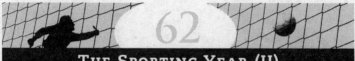

THE SPORTING YEAR (II)

In which year did ...

1.   Liverpool finish runners-up to Everton in the First Division Championship, Last Suspect win the Grand National and Manchester United win the FA Cup?

2.   Liverpool win the Charity Shield, Anglo win the Grand National and Real Madrid win the European Cup?

3.   Liverpool finish runners-up to Arsenal in the First Division Championship, Boris Becker win the Wimbledon Men's Singles and Jocky Wilson win the BDO World Darts Championship?

THE SPORTING YEAR (II)

4. Liverpool win the European Cup and the First Division Championship, and Martina Navratilova win the Wimbledon Ladies' Singles ?

5. Steven Gerrard sign for Liverpool as a trainee, Earth Summit win the Grand National and John Higgins win the World Snooker Championships?

6. Liverpool beat Everton in the FA Cup Final, West Tip win the Grand National and Steaua Bucharest win the European Championship?

THE SPORTING YEAR (II)

7. Liverpool lose to Arsenal in the League Cup Final, John Lowe win the BDO World Darts Championship and Steve Davis win the World Snooker Championship?

8. Liverpool win the League Cup, Richie Burness win the BDO World Darts Championship and Stephen Hendry win the World Snooker Championship?

9. Gary McAllister leave Liverpool to join Coventry City, Bindaree win the Grand National and Surrey win the County Championship?

10. Liverpool win the First Division Championship, Essex win the County Championship and Hamburg win the European Cup?

KENNY DALGLISH (II)

1. Which club did Kenny grow up supporting as a young boy?

2. How many First Division Championship medals did Kenny win during his time at Anfield?

3. Can you name any three seasons in which Kenny won a First Division Championship medal during his time as a player with the Reds?

4. In his early days at Glasgow Celtic, Kenny was farmed out to the club's nursery side. Can you name the United in question?

5. How much did Kenny cost the Reds – £440,000, £540,000 or £640,000?

KENNY DALGLISH (II)

6. In which year was Kenny voted the English Football Writers' Player of the Year?

7. Which legendary Brazilian footballer presented Kenny with the English Football Writers' Player of the Year Award?

8. In which year did Kenny's playing career with the Reds come to an end?

9. Which club did Kenny manage from 1997 to 1998?

10. How many Scottish First Championships did Kenny win with Celtic?

64

EMLYN HUGHES

1. In which year did Emlyn sign for Liverpool?

2. How many League appearances did Emlyn make for the Reds – 464, 474 or 484?

3. Emlyn later became a director of a City Football Club. Can you name the club concerned?

4. Prior to signing for Liverpool, which North-West club did Emlyn play for?

5. In his Anfield career, how many League goals did Emlyn score for the Reds – 30, 35 or 40?

EMLYN HUGHES

6. In which position did Emlyn play most of his games for the Reds?

7. After leaving Anfield, which team did Emlyn sign for?

8. Which United did Emlyn once manage?

9. Emlyn made an appearance in a comic strip for a fictional football team, but what was the name of the team?

10. In which year did he leave Liverpool?

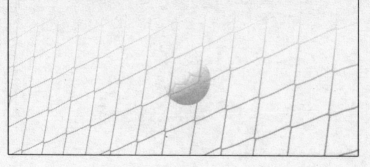

FA CUP WINNERS 1973/74

1. Which team did the Reds beat
    at Wembley in 1973/74 to lift
    the FA Cup for the second
    time?

2. Liverpool beat which Rovers in
    Round 3?

3. Who scored the Reds' winning
    goal in a 1–0 FA Cup quarter-
    final victory?

4. Can you recall the score in the
    Final?

5. Which City did Liverpool beat
    in the semi-finals?

FA CUP WINNERS 1973/74

6. Name the manager who guided the Reds to FA Cup glory in 1973/74.

7. Can you recall which United took the Reds to a replay in Round 4 before the Reds finally progressed to Round 5?

8. How many of Liverpool's 1973/74 FA Cup ties went to a replay?

9. Can you name the team, which would go on to win the FA Cup in 1978, which Liverpool beat in Round 5?

10. Name any Liverpool player who scored in the 1973/74 inal.

LEAGUE CHAMPIONS 1975/76

1. To the nearest five, how many points did the Reds end the season with?

2. The Reds lost 2–0 away to a London side on the opening day of the season. Can you name them?

3. Against which United did the Reds record their first League away win of the season?

4. Can you name the North-East club which was the last team to beat the Reds in the League in the 1975/76 season?

5. How many of their 21 League home games did Liverpool win?

LEAGUE CHAMPIONS 1975/76

6. Who finished the season as the Reds' top League goal scorer with 16 goals?

7. Liverpool won away on the last day of the League season to clinch the First Division Championship but can you name the side they defeated?

8. Can you name the City with which the Reds drew 1–1 away on Boxing Day?

9. Can you name the winger who scored the Reds' first League goal of the season?

10. How many of their 42 League games did Liverpool lose on their way to winning the 1975/76 First Division Championship?

GRAEME SOUNESS (I)

1. In which year did Graeme sign for Liverpool?

2. How many League appearances did Graeme make for the Reds – 247, 267 or 287?

3. Graeme went on to play for which Italian team after leaving Anfield?

4. Prior to signing for the Reds, which club did Souness play for?

5. In his Anfield career, how many League goals did Graeme score for the Reds – 18, 28 or 38?

GRAEME SOUNESS (I)

6. In which position did Graeme normally play for the Reds?

7. Of which club was Graeme the player-manager from 1986 to 1991?

8. Graeme once managed a Turkish club, but which one?

9. In which year was Graeme appointed the manager of Liverpool?

10. During the 1996/97 season, which club did Graeme manage?

PHIL THOMPSON (I)

1. In which year did Phil sign for Liverpool?

2. How many League appearances did Phil make for the Reds – 340, 360 or 380?

3. How old was Phil when he made his League début for the Reds – 18, 19 or 20?

4. Phil went on to play for which Yorkshire club after leaving Anfield?

5. In his Anfield career, how many League goals did Phil score for the Reds – 7, 17 or 27?

PHIL THOMPSON (I)

6. Can you recall the player Phil succeeded as Liverpool captain?

7. Against which United did Phil make his début for the Reds?

8. Which job was Phil given at Liverpool after he quit playing football?

9. When Gerrard Houllier was appointed the manager of Liverpool, what job was Phil given?

10. What was Phil's greatest accomplishment as the captain of Liverpool?

UEFA CUP WINNERS 1975/76

1. Which team did the Reds beat in the Final of the 1975/76 UEFA Cup?

2. Liverpool beat which Scottish side in Round 1 of the competition?

3. Who scored the Reds' first hat-trick in their successful 1975/76 UEFA Cup campaign?

4. Can you recall the aggregate score in the Final?

5. Which Spanish club did Liverpool beat in the semi-finals?

69

UEFA CUP WINNERS 1975/76

6. Name the manager who guided the Reds to UEFA Cup glory in 1975/76.

7. Can you recall the East German club which the Reds beat over two legs in Round 4?

8. How many of their 12 1975/76 UEFA Cup ties did the Reds lose?

9. Can you name the Polish team which the Reds beat home and away in Round 3?

10. Name any two of the three Liverpool players who scored in either leg of the 1975/76 UEFA Cup Final.

WHO ARE WE PLAYING? (IV)

1. If Liverpool were in opposition against the Imps, which City would they be playing?

2. If Liverpool were in opposition against the Baggies, which Midlands club would they be playing?

3. If Liverpool were in opposition against the Rams, who would they be playing?

4. If Liverpool were in opposition against the Vikings, which Rovers would they be playing?

5. If Liverpool were in opposition against the Terriers, which Town would they be playing?

WHO ARE WE PLAYING? (IV)

6. If Liverpool were in opposition against the Eagles, who would they be playing?

7. If Liverpool were in opposition against the Tractor Boys, who would they be playing?

8. If Liverpool were in opposition against the Monkey Hangers, who would they be playing?

9. If Liverpool were in opposition against the Silkmen, which Town would they be playing?

10. If Liverpool were in opposition against the Fleet, who would they be playing?

GÉRARD HOULLIER

1. As part of his English degree, Gérard spent a year in Liverpool (1969–70) and worked as an Assistant at Alsop Comprehensive School. He attended his first ever Liverpool game on 16 September 1969 but can you recall the name of the Irish side the Reds thrashed 10–0 at Anfield?

2. In which year did Gérard take charge of Liverpool?

3. Who did Gérard succeed as the manager of Liverpool?

4. Can you name the French side Gérard guided to the French national Championship, Le Championnat, in season 1985/86?

5. Gérard was the manager of which team in 1992 before resigning in 1993?

GÉRARD HOULLIER

6. In October 2001, Gérard fell ill at Anfield during a Premier League match and was rushed to hospital where he underwent an 11-hour emergency heart operation. Can you recall Liverpool's Premiership opponents that day?

7. What was the first trophy Liverpool won under the management of Gérard?

8. In which year did Gérard leave his position as boss of the Reds?

9. Gérard was appointed manager of which team in May 2005, guiding them to two successive French Championships in seasons 2005/06 and 2006/07?

10. What was the last trophy Liverpool won under the management of Gérard?

PLAYERS (II)

1. Who captained Liverpool to FA Cup glory in 1974?

2. How many times did Graeme Souness guide Rangers to Scottish Championship success?

3. Jamie Redknapp scored the Reds' 450th Premiership goal on 5 May 1999 against which team who knocked them out of the FA Cup earlier in the season?

4. In which year did Markus Babbel leave Anfield?

5. Who was the top goal scorer for the Reds in their successful 1964/65 FA Cup campaign?

PLAYERS (II)

6. Which Reds defender scored Liverpool's first goal of their 1975/76 League Cup campaign from the penalty spot?

7. Who, on 24 September 2005, became the second Liverpool goalkeeper to score an own-goal in the FA Premier League?

8. In the 1999/2000 season, which Australian club was Ian Rush playing for?

9. After leaving Liverpool, which North-Esastern club did Phil Boersma sign for?

10. Prior to signing for Liverpool, which Danish club did Daniel Agger play for?

MIXED BAG (II)

1. Who did Graeme Souness succeed as Liverpool manager?

2. Which club did Liverpool beat in the 2006 FA Community Shield?

3. How many games did Liverpool play in the competition en route to winning the FA Cup in 1965?

4. Name either of the teams Liverpool beat after a replay during their 1976/77 FA Cup campaign?

5. In which position did Gary Ablett usually play for Liverpool?

6. On 27 May 1976, the Reds lost 3–1 away to which Spanish team who share the same

73

MIXED BAG (II)

name as a Greek mythological character, the son of Jupiter?

7. How many League Cups did the Reds win at the Millennium Stadium?

8. How many League goals did Xabi Alonso score in the 2005/06 season for the Reds?

9. Can you name the Liverpool captain who took the European Cup down to his local pub, The Falcon, in Kirkby, so as his mates could have their photographs taken with it?

10. A number of years after he left Anfield for the second time in his career, Ian Rush was appointed manager of which City?

74

STEVE HEIGHWAY

1. In 1970, which Lancashire United did Steve play for while attending a university course in Economics?

2. In which capital city was Steve born?

3. Can you recall the United Steve made his début against for the Reds?

4. How many European trophies did Steve win at Anfield with the Reds?

5. During his Anfield career, how many League goals did Steve score – 30, 40 or 50?

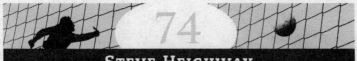

74

STEVE HEIGHWAY

6. Can you recall how many international caps Steve won – 33, 35 or 37?

7. In all competitions, how many appearances did he make for the Reds – 475, 500 or 525?

8. Steve was offered and accepted an important job with Liverpool in 1989. Which position did he take up?

9. How many League Championships did Steve win with Liverpool?

10. How many times did Steve win a European Cup winners' medal with the Reds?

RAFAEL BENÍTEZ

1. Can you name the famous Spanish club's youth team which Rafa played for in 1974?

2. After retiring as a football player, Rafa became a manager. Which one of Real Madrid's junior teams did he take charge of from 1986 to 1989?

3. Rafa guided 'Los Ches' to Primera Liga success in 2001/02 and 2003/04. By which name are 'Los Ches' better known?

4. Of which 'Real' was Rafa appointed the manager in 1995?

5. In 1996, of which club was Rafa appointed manager?

RAFAEL BENÍTEZ

6. In 1981, Rafa left Real Madrid to sign for which Spanish club in the Tercera Division?

7. What was the first major trophy Rafa guided the Reds to success in?

8. Can you name the Segunda Liga side, and popular holiday resort for British holidaymakers, which Rafa managed in season 2000/01, leading them into the Primera Liga?

9. With which club was Rafa linked in 2005/06 but decided to remain at Anfield?

10. In which Cup competition did Rafa guide his team to success in season 2003/04?

REDS AT THE WORLD CUP (III)

1. Who was the only Liverpool player to score for his country at the 1978 World Cup Finals in Spain?

2. How many Liverpool players played at least one game at the 1974 World Cup Finals?

3. Can you name the Liverpool player who played for Scotland in the 1990 World Cup Finals?

4. Which Liverpool player conceded six goals at the 2002 World Cup Finals before being dropped by his country?

5. How many different countries were represented by Liverpool players at the 2006 World Cup Finals?

76

REDS AT THE WORLD CUP (III)

6. Name two of Liverpool's three Republic of Ireland players who played in the 1990 World Cup Finals in Italy.

7. How many former Liverpool players or managers have managed a team at the World Cup Finals?

8. Which Liverpool goalkeeper conceded a goal at the 1998 World Cup Finals in France?

9. How many different countries were represented by Liverpool players at the 2006 World Cup Finals?

10. Name two of Liverpool's three England players who played in the 1990 World Cup Finals in Italy.

THE TROPHY YEARS

1. In which year did Liverpool win a trophy, John McEnroe win his first Wimbledon Men's Singles title, Chris Everett Lloyd become the Ladies' Champion, Bill Rogers win the British Golf Open, Aldaniti win the Grand National, and the Oakland Raiders win Superbowl XV?

2. In which year did Liverpool win a trophy, the West Indies beat England in the Cricket World Cup Final, Jody Scheckter win the F1 World Championship, Nottingham Forest win the European Cup and Terry Griffiths win his only World Snooker Championship?

3. In which year did Liverpool win a trophy, Nick Faldo win the British Golf Open, Leeds United win the First Division Championship, Party Politics win the Grand National, Pakistan win the Cricket World Cup,

THE TROPHY YEARS

Nigel Mansell win the F1 World Championship and Barcelona host the Olympic Games?

4. In which year did Liverpool win a trophy, Calgary host the Olympic Winter Games, Stefan Edberg and Steffi Graf become Wimbledon Champions, Holland win Football's European Championships and Seve Ballesteros win the British Golf Open?

5. In which year did Liverpool win the Double, Argentina become World Cup winners, West Tip win the Grand National, Alain Prost win the F1 World Championship, Greg Norman win the British Golf Open and the Chicago Bears win Superbowl XX?

6. In which year did Liverpool win a trophy, Italy win the World Cup, Keke Rosberg become the F1 World Champion, Aston Villa win the European Cup,

THE TROPHY YEARS

Jimmy Connors and Martina Navratilova rule Wimbledon, Grittar win the Grand National and Alex Higgins win his second World Snooker Championship?

7. In which year did Liverpool win the European Cup, Hallo Dandy win the Grand National, Niki Lauda became F1 World Champion, Sarajevo host the Olympic Winter Games, France win Football's European Championships and the Los Angeles Raiders win Superbowl XVIII?

8. In which year did Liverpool win a trophy, Southampton win the FA Cup, Czechoslovakia win the European Football Championships, Montreal host the Olympic Games and Raymond Floyd win the US Masters?

77

THE TROPHY YEARS

9. In which year did Liverpool win a trophy, Moscow host the Olympic Games, Lake Placid host the Olympic Winter Games, West Germany win the European Football Championships, Björn Borg win his last Men's Singles title at Wimbledon and the Pittsburgh Steelers win Superbowl XIV?

10. In which year did Liverpool win a trophy, Virginia Wade win the Ladies' Singles title at Wimbledon, Manchester United win the FA Cup, Niki Lauda win the F1 World Championship, Red Rum win his third Grand National and John Spencer become World Snooker Champion?

78

RAY CLEMENCE

1. How many League appearances did Ray make for the Reds – 460, 470 or 480?

2. Can you recall the year in which Liverpool signed Ray?

3. Prior to signing for the Reds, which team did Ray play for?

4. In which year did Ray make his League début for Liverpool?

5. After leaving Anfield, which London club did Ray sign for?

6. How old was Ray when he made his League début for the Reds?

78

RAY CLEMENCE

7. In which year during the early 1980s did Ray leave Anfield?

8. Ray Clemence captained England only once during his international career. Can you name the South American team to which England lost 1–0 on 12 May 1981?

9. Can you name the Doug, a former team-mate of Ray's at Liverpool, who was co-manager with Ray at Tottenham in season 1992/93?

10. On 2 February 2005, what did Ray announce he had been diagnosed with?

PAST MASTERS (I)

1. In which season did Alan Hansen establish himself in the Liverpool starting XI?

2. Which Rovers did Ian St John play for in the 1972/73 season?

3. Name the defender who made his Liverpool début against Everton at Goodison Park on 9 October 1974 in place of the injured Alec Lindsay.

4. By which nickname was Mark Lawrenson known?

5. Which Red, along with Stanley Matthews, was the only player selected for the Great Britain Representative sides in 1947 and 1955?

79

PAST MASTERS (I)

6. Name either of the Reds players who scored in Liverpool's 1975/76 FA Cup campaign.

7. How many goals did Bob Paisley score for the Reds – 2, 12 or 22?

8. At which Danish club did Jan Mølby begin his professional football career?

9. Which record does Elisha Scott hold at Liverpool FC?

10. The following banner appeared at the 1977 European Cup Final in Rome and can now be found in the Liverpool FC Museum: 'X Ate The Frogs Legs, Made The Swiss Roll, Now He's Munching Gladbach'. Who was 'X'?

LIVERPOOL'S ENGLAND CAPTAINS

1. Which Red captained England for the first and only time in his career against Israel on 13 February 1988?

2. With which club did Kevin Keegan win 16 caps as the England captain?

3. Can you name the country England lost 1–0 to when Steven Gerrard captained the national team on 31 March 2004?

4. Who was the last Liverpool player to be appointed the England captain, excluding single internationals or taking over the armband when the captain left the field?

5. Prior to the player named in question 4, who was the previous Liverpool player to be appointed the England captain, excluding games where a player took over the armband when the captain left the field?

LIVERPOOL'S ENGLAND CAPTAINS

6. Which future Liverpool player, then at Derby County, captained England against the USSR on 23 May 1991?

7. In how many internationals did Michael Owen captain England while he was a Liverpool player?

8. Prior to Michael Owen, who was the last Liverpool player to captain England while playing for three different clubs?

9. Which Red captained England for the first and only time in his career against Iceland on 2 June 1982?

10. Can you name the Liverpool player who was England's first post-World War II captain?

BRUCE GROBBELAAR (I)

1. Prior to signing for Liverpool, which Canadian team did Bruce play for?

2. In which country was Bruce born?

3. Can you recall the Liverpool team-mate Bruce verbally attacked during the 1986 FA Cup Final?

4. Before moving to Liverpool, Bruce was at which other English club on loan?

5. Name the Liverpool legend who preceded Bruce in the Liverpool goal.

BRUCE GROBBELAAR (I)

6. Can you recall the first piece of silverware which Bruce Grobbelaar won with the Reds?

7. During his time at Liverpool, Bruce was loaned to a City. Can you name them?

8. Can you recall the name of the newspaper that accused Bruce and others of match-fixing?

9. After leaving Liverpool, which south-coast club did Bruce sign for?

10. How many League appearances did Bruce make for the Reds – 400, 440 or 480?

THREE LIONS ON A SHIRT (I)

1. Up to and including England's 3–2 loss to Croatia on 21 November 2007, name either of the 2 other clubs to have supplied more England goal scorers than Liverpool.

2. Name any four of the Liverpool players who played for England against Albania on 5 September 2001.

3. Who in 1998 became the 50th Liverpool player to be capped by England?

4. Who was the last Red to be capped by England during the 1950s?

5. Can you name the Liverpool player who was England's first post-World War II international?

THREE LIONS ON A SHIRT (I)

6. In 2000, which Red became the 1,099th player to be capped by England?

7. Name the legendary Red who won his one and only England cap in 1971.

8. Can you name any of the three Reds who won their first England cap in the same international in 1963?

9. How many Liverpool players started for England against Switzerland on 7 September 1977?

10. Name the Rabbi who was capped by England in 1899.

AWAY DAYS (III)

1. If Liverpool visited Craven Cottage, which team would they be playing away?

2. If Liverpool visited Portman Road, which team would they be playing away?

3. If Liverpool visited Belle Vue, which Rovers would they be playing away?

4. If Liverpool visited Blundell Park, which Town would they be playing away?

5. If Liverpool visited St James' Park, which City would they be playing away?

AWAY DAYS (III)

6. If Liverpool visited KitKat Crescent, which City would they be playing away?

7. If Liverpool visited Elland Road, which team would they be playing away?

8. If Liverpool visited Priestfield Stadium, which team would they be playing away?

9. If Liverpool visited Brisbane Road, which team would they be playing away?

10. If Liverpool visited the Williamson Motors Stadium, which team would they be playing away?

84

MARK LAWRENSON

1. At which Lancashire club did Mark begin his professional football career?

2. Prior to signing for the Reds, which Sussex-based club did Mark play for?

3. To the nearest 50, how many League appearances did Mark make for Liverpool?

4. In which year during the early 1980s did Mark move to Anfield?

5. How much did Liverpool pay for the services of Mark – £800,000, £900,000 or £1.0m?

84

MARK LAWRENSON

6. How many League goals did Mark score for the Reds – 1, 11 or 21?

7. In which year in the late 1980s did Mark leave Anfield?

8. Although he was born in England, which country did Mark play international football for during his career?

9. Since his playing days, what does Mark work as?

10. How many full international caps did Mark win – 39, 49 or 59?

THE LIVERPOOL FC QUIZ BOOK

85

BILLY LIDDELL

1. Can you name the Scottish city
    in which Billy was born?

2. Name the Scottish League side
    Billy turned down a move to in
    favour of joining the Reds.

3. Can you name the Liverpool
    manager who brought Billy to
    Anfield?

4. In which of Britain's armed
    forces did Billy serve during
    World War II?

5. Can you recall Liverpool's
    opponents when Billy made
    his scoring club début –
    Chester City, Chesterfield or
    Colchester United?

BILLY LIDDELL

6. How many appearances did Billy make for Liverpool – 434, 534 or 634?

7. In his first full season at Anfield, Billy played alongside a future Liverpool manager. Can you name him?

8. What was the first winners' medal Billy picked up during his Anfield career?

9. How many full international caps did he win for Scotland – 18, 28 or 38?

10. How many FA Cup Finals did Billy play in for the Reds?

PHIL NEAL

1. How many League appearances did Phil make for the Reds – 355, 455 or 555?

2. In which year did Liverpool sign Phil?

3. How old was Phil when he made his League début for Liverpool – 19, 21 or 23?

4. Prior to moving to Anfield, which Town did Phil play for?

5. To the nearest 10, how many League goals did Phil score for the Reds?

PHIL NEAL

6. Can you recall the year in which Phil left Anfield?

7. What was the last trophy Phil won with Liverpool?

8. After leaving Anfield, which Wanderers did Phil sign for?

9. Which player was Phil bought to replace?

10. Can you name the Welsh side Phil used to manage?

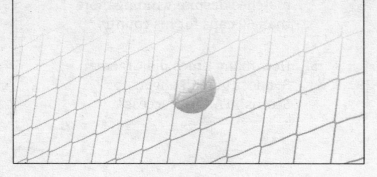

PAST MASTERS (II)

1. At which United did Peter Beardsley begin his professional football career in England?

2. Can you recall for how many seasons Billy Liddell was the Reds' leading goal scorer?

3. Which Red played in Liverpool's first five European Cup Finals?

4. Can you name the former Liverpool player who only played a total of 26 minutes for England in World Cup Finals matches despite winning more than 60 caps for his country?

5. How many times did Graeme Souness guide Rangers to Scottish FA Cup success?

PAST MASTERS (II)

6. Mark Lawrenson was formerly a defensive coach for which FA Premier League side?

7. Who scored a hat-trick for the Reds in Round 3 of their successful 1975/76 UEFA Cup campaign?

8. What was the first trophy Alan Hansen won with the Reds?

9. In which year did Phil Boersma leave Anfield?

10. Name the winger who made his Liverpool début against Everton at Goodison Park on 9 October 1974.

88

EUROPEAN LANDMARK GOALS

1. Which striker scored the Reds' 50th goal in Europe versus TSV Munchen on 7 November 1967?

2. Name the World Cup-winning player from 1990 who scored the Reds' 100th away goal in Europe versus FC Kosice.

3. Which winger scored the Reds' 100th goal in Europe versus Dynamo Berlin on 13 December 1972?

4. Which midfielder scored the Reds' 150th goal in Europe versus FC Bruges on 28 April 1976?

5. Which Liverpool defender, who wasn't noted for his goal-scoring ability, found the back of the net on 19 December 1978 against Anderlecht to claim the Reds' 200th European goal?

EUROPEAN LANDMARK GOALS

6. Can you name the England international who scored the Reds' 250th home goal in Europe versus FC Haka?

7. Which full-back scored the Reds' 250th goal in Europe versus JK Helsinki on 2 November 1982?

8. Can you name the Welshman who scored the Reds' 300th goal in Europe versus FC Tirol on 11 December 1991?

9. Which England international midfielder scored the Reds' 350th goal in Europe versus Rapid Bucharest on 14 September 2000?

10. The Reds' 400th goal in Europe against Spartak Moscow was scored by an England international on 2 October 2002. Can you name him?

BOB PAISLEY OBE

1. Which job did Bob have at Liverpool before he was made a coach at Anfield?

2. Which winners' medal did Bob pick up in the 1938/39 season?

3. Which non-league club was Bob playing for when he collected the medal in 1938/39?

4. In which year did Bob sign for the Reds?

5. Can you name the manager who brought Bob to Anfield?

BOB PAISLEY OBE

6. In which year did he make his début for the Reds?

7. How many appearances did Bob make for the Reds – 277, 287 or 297?

8. Which was Bob's last season as a player?

9. In which year did Bob succeed Bill Shankly as the manager of Liverpool?

10. Can you recall the first trophy Liverpool won under Bob's management?

STEVEN GERRARD

1. In which year did Steven make his Liverpool début?

2. Steven was a Liverpool fan as a kid, but in his autobiography he admitted to wearing the football top of a rival team. Which team was it?

3. Which shirt number does Steven normally wear for England?

4. By which nickname is Steven better known?

5. Has Steven been awarded a CBE, an MBE or an OBE?

6. Can you recall England's opponents when Steven captained the team in place of the injured John Terry in a 3–2

90

STEVEN GERRARD

defeat at the new Wembley on 21 November 2007, ending England's chances of qualifying for the 2008 European Football Championships?

7. What number did Steven wear for the Reds prior to his existing Number 8 jersey?

8. Against which Rovers did Steven make his League début for Liverpool?

9. What is Steven's middle name?

10. Name the club Steven was linked with a move to prior to the start of the 2005/06 season.

THE REDS' WELSH DRAGONS

1. Which Red played for both Cardiff City and Swansea City?

2. In all competitions, how many goals did Dean Saunders score for the Reds – 15, 20 or 25?

3. Which Red won a record 72 caps for Wales, although this has subsequently been surpassed?

4. To the nearest five, how many Merseyside derby goals did Ian Rush score?

5. Which former Red scored two goals in the 1993/94 League Cup Final to help his side to a 3–1 win over the Treble-seeking Manchester United?

THE REDS' WELSH DRAGONS

6. Can you name the former Welsh Red who managed St Etienne in season 2000/01?

7. In the late 1970s, which Red was sold back to the same Welsh club that Liverpool had purchased him from, for £100,000 more than the Reds paid for him?

8. Against which Welsh side did Ian Rush score twice in a 3–0 away win in an English First Division game on 18 September 1982?

9. Name the Liverpool striker who scored for the Reds in a 3–0 home win against Swansea City on 23 January 1971.

10. Which Red was the first player to win five League Cup winners' medals?

THE MERSEYSIDE DERBY (V)

1. In which famous Merseyside derby did Ian Rush break the legendary Dixie Dean's Merseyside derby goal-scoring record?

2. Why did the players not do the traditional lap of honour around Wembley Stadium following Liverpool's 3–2 extra-time win over Everton in the 1989 FA Cup Final?

3. What was of historic significance about Everton's fifth-round second replay 1–0 win over Liverpool in the FA Cup on 27 February 1991?

4. In which year during the late 1890s did Everton first lose to Liverpool in a Merseyside derby League match?

5. Which legendary Reds goalkeeper did Everton almost sign in 1934 for £250? The move was scrapped when Liverpool fans protested to the *Liverpool Echo*.

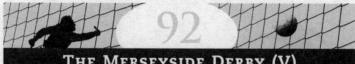

THE MERSEYSIDE DERBY (V)

6. Which 'Challenge' Cup was contested from 1957 to 1962 to keep the derby fixture alive while Liverpool were in Division Two?

7. Which Liverpool player appeared to handle a shot on the goal line in the 1984 Merseyside League Cup Final at Wembley Stadium?

8. Who was fined £60,000 by Liverpool and the Premier League in 1999 after he mimed snorting cocaine off the white line of the penalty box to celebrate a goal against Everton?

9. In 1966, Bill Shankly lost out to Everton in his attempt to sign this player, quipping, 'Don't worry. At least you'll be able to play close to a great team.' Who was Shankly's quip directed at?

10. Which former Everton player was the first to be signed by Kenny Dalglish in September 1985?

93

ROBBIE FOWLER

1. Robbie enjoyed two spells at Anfield, but in which year did his first spell commence?

2. Can you name the club Robbie signed for after he left Anfield for a second time?

3. When Robbie first left Anfield in 2001, which club did he join?

4. From which club did the Reds re-sign Robbie?

5. To the nearest 20, how many League goals did Robbie score for Liverpool?

93

ROBBIE FOWLER

6. To the nearest £2.0m, how much did the Reds receive for Robbie in 2001?

7. Which club did Robbie support as a young boy?

8. How many full international caps did Robbie win for England – 16, 26 or 36?

9. Can you name the side Robbie joined in 2008?

10. Which Top 1,000 list, published by the *Sunday Times*, did Robbie's name appear in?

94

PLAYERS (III)

1. Apart from Graeme Souness, can you name the other Red who appeared on TV in a 1982 episode of Alan Bleasdale's *Boys from the Blackstuff*?

2. Can you name the English Red who played for Team America in the 1976 USA Bicentennial Cup tournament matches against England and Brazil?

3. Which former player, and later a very successful manager with one of the club's greatest rivals, was the first person connected with the club to appear on the popular TV show *This Is Your Life* when he was honoured on 12 May 1971?

4. Which former Red has appeared on TV in advertisements for Wash & Go shampoo?

PLAYERS (III)

5. In 1925, which goalkeeper became the first player from outside the UK and Ireland to play for the Reds?

6. Name the Liverpool striker who was awarded the PFA Merit Award in 1997.

7. Only four players have scored five goals for Liverpool in a game. Can you name any three of the four?

8. Name the Scottish Red who was awarded the Football Writers' Association Footballer of the Year Award in 1989.

9. Name the Red who was on the losing side in FA Cup Finals with three different teams.

10. On 17 May 1980, which Red became the first Liverpool player to score an own-goal playing for England?

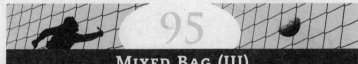

MIXED BAG (III)

1. On 4 December 1909, which United led 5–2 at Anfield, only to see Liverpool come storming back to win the game 6–5?

2. Which team award, inaugurated in 1960, did Liverpool win in 1977, 1986 and 2001?

3. Which future Red won the 1981 Professional Football Association's Players' Player of the Year Award?

4. Who scored the Reds' last FA Premier League goal of 2006?

5. Who was the first Liverpool player to captain England?

6. What were unveiled at Anfield on 26 August 1982?

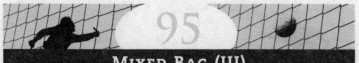

MIXED BAG (III)

7. What was the name given to Liverpool's match programme for the visit of Norwich City to Anfield on 30 April 1994 in a match marking the last ever game in front of the old standing Kop?

8. Who succeeded Phil Neal as the captain of Liverpool?

9. On 3 June 2003, England beat Serbia & Montenegro 2–1 at the Walkers Stadium in a game which saw four different players wear England's captain's armband. Can you name any two of the three Liverpool players who captained England in the game?

10. Can you name the Red who had to wait a record 11 years and 49 days, excluding games missed by players as a result of either World War, between the time he was awarded his first cap by England and his second?

AWARDS (I)

1. Can you name the Liverpool defender who was awarded the Football Writers' Association Footballer of the Year Award in 1977?

2. Name the Liverpool goalkeeper who was awarded the PFA Merit Award in 1998.

3. Can you name the former Liverpool manager who was awarded the PFA Merit Award in 1978?

4. The Football Writers' Tribute Award is presented on an annual basis to an individual whom the Football Writers' Committee feels has made an outstanding contribution to the national game. Which Red won it in 1984?

5. Name any year in which Robbie Fowler won the PFA Young Player of the Year Award.

AWARDS (I)

6. Which future Red won the 2000 PFA Young Player of the Year Award?

7. Name the Liverpool player who was awarded the Football Writers' Association Footballer of the Year Award in 1988 and in 1990.

8. Who is the only Liverpool player to win the coveted European Player of the Year Award otherwise known as the Ballon d'Or (Golden Ball)?

9. Name the young Red who was the first Liverpool player to win the PFA Young Player of the Year Award.

10. Which Liverpool player won the 1983 Professional Football Association's Players' Player of the Year Award?

TV STARS

1. Who played for the Reds and during his football career appeared in TV advertisements for Brut Aftershave, Dentyne Chewing Gum and Sugar Puffs?

2. Which former Red has appeared on TV in an advertisement for Carlsberg in which he played a butler?

3. In 1982, Graeme Souness appeared on TV in an episode of Alan Bleasdale's *Boys from the Blackstuff*. Can you recall the name of the character played by Bernard Hill who approached Souness in a bar and said, 'You look like me...'?

4. Can you name the Liverpool legend who appeared on the popular TV show *This Is Your Life* when he has honoured on 28 December 1977?

5. Which former Red is the only England footballer to have captained a team for

TV STARS

a complete series of BBC TV's *A Question of Sport*?

6.   Which Red, during his football career, appeared in TV advertisements for Lucozade, Nationwide Building Society and Walkers Crisps?

7.   Which Liverpool legend appeared on the TV show *This is Your Life* on 10 January 1973?

8.   Which Liverpool striker appeared on *This is Your Life* on 14 February 1979?

9.   Which former Red has appeared on TV in advertisements for the *Daily Telegraph*?

10. On 16 February 1983, who became the first Red still playing for the club to appear on the popular TV show *This Is Your Life*?

ROY EVANS

1. In which position did Roy play his 11 first-team games for Liverpool?

2. During the summer of 1973, Roy played in which overseas League while on loan from Liverpool?

3. Which managerial post did Bill Shankly give to Roy in the early 1970s?

4. How many different Liverpool managers did Roy work under at Anfield in a coaching/training capacity before he was finally appointed the manager of Liverpool?

5. Can you recall either of Roy's middle names – one beginning with the letter 'Q' and the other with an 'E'?

ROY EVANS

6. In which year was Roy appointed the manager of Liverpool?

7. What was the only trophy Liverpool won under Roy's management?

8. Can you recall the man Liverpool brought in to assist Roy at Anfield as joint-manager of the club?

9. In 2004, Roy teamed up with a former Liverpool legend as the assistant manager of which side?

10. In February 2007, Roy began working as a part-time assistant to manager Brian Carey at which Welsh club?

DOUBLE WINNERS 1985/86 (I)

1. How many points did the Reds end the season with?

2. Which team did Liverpool beat in the 1985/86 FA Cup Final to clinch the Double?

3. The Reds beat which London club 2–0 at Anfield on the opening day of the season?

4. At which London ground did the Reds win their FA Cup semi-final?

5. Liverpool disposed of which 1984 FA Cup runners-up after a replay in Round 6?

DOUBLE WINNERS 1985/86 (I)

6. Can you name the United that was the first team to beat the Reds in the League during the season?

7. How many FA Cup goals did Ian Rush score in the 1985/86 competition?

8. Which team did Liverpool beat on the last League day of the season to clinch the First Division Championship?

9. Name the two players who scored for the Reds in the 1985/86 FA Cup Final.

10. The Reds lost 1–0 away to which Lancashire club on Boxing Day 1985?

JOHN TOSHACK

1. John managed the same Spanish club on three separate occasions. Can you name them?

2. To the nearest 25, how many League appearances did John make for Liverpool?

3. Prior to signing for the Reds, which Welsh club did John play for?

4. In which year did John move to Anfield?

5. How many League goals did John score for Liverpool – 74, 79 or 83?

100

JOHN TOSHACK

6. After leaving the Reds, which Welsh club did John sign for?

7. Which national team did John take charge of in 1994 for one game?

8. How many international goals did John score for Wales – 10, 12 or 15?

9. Can you name the Welsh club managed by John from 1978 to 1984?

10. Name the club John managed from 1989/90 and then again for a brief second spell in 1999.

EUROPEAN CUP WINNERS 1977/78

1. Which team did Liverpool beat in the 1978 European Cup Final?

2. Name the East German club Liverpool met in the first round of the competition.

3. Which city hosted the 1984 European Cup Final?

4. Can you recall the Reds' highest aggregate win in the 1977/78 competition?

5. Name the German side the Reds beat in the semi-final.

6. Can you recall the Portuguese side Liverpool beat en route to lifting the European Cup in 1978?

EUROPEAN CUP WINNERS 1977/78

7. How many of their seven games in the 1977/78 competition did the Reds lose?

8. Who was the Reds' leading goal scorer in their successful 1977/78 European Cup campaign?

9. Name any two of the three goal scorers for the Reds in their 3–0 semi-final win at Anfield.

10. Can you recall the manager who guided Liverpool to European Cup Final success in season 1977/78?

102

UEFA CUP WINNERS 1972/73

1. Which team, and future European Cup runners-up to the Reds, did the Reds beat in the 1972/73 UEFA Cup Final?

2. Which West German team, and European Cup runners-up in 1959/60, did Liverpool beat in Round 1 of the competition?

3. Who scored the most goals for the Reds in their successful 1972/73 UEFA Cup campaign?

4. Can you recall the aggregate score in the Final?

5. Which English club did Liverpool beat in the semi-final?

UEFA CUP WINNERS 1972/73

6. Name the player who captained the Reds to UEFA Cup glory in 1972/73.

7. Can you recall the East German club which the Reds beat home and away in Round 4?

8. How many of their 12 1972/73 UEFA Cup ties did the Reds lose?

9. Can you name the Greek side that the Reds beat home and away in Round 2?

10. Name the two Liverpool players who scored in the first leg of the Reds' 3–0 win in the 1972/73 UEFA Cup Final.

ALMOST MADE IT SIX IN 2006/07

1. Can you name the Turkish side who finished bottom of Liverpool's group, Group C?

2. How many of their six group games did Liverpool win?

3. Which French side finished third behind Liverpool in Group C?

4. Can you name the Spanish team that Liverpool put out of the competition on the away-goals rule in the first knockout round?

5. Liverpool's Peter Crouch was the second highest goal scorer in the 2006/07 UEFA Champions League behind AC Milan's Kaka who scored 10 goals. How many times did Crouch find the back of the net?

ALMOST MADE IT SIX IN 2006/07

6. Liverpool beat this Dutch team, earlier runners-up to Liverpool in Group C, in the quarter-finals. Can you name them?

7. Who were Liverpool's semi-final opponents?

8. What was the aggregate score after the two semi-final leg ties?

9. In which city was the 2007 UEFA Champions League Final played?

10. Liverpool lost 2–1 to AC Milan in the Final. Who scored Liverpool's solitary goal?

EUROPEAN SUPER CUP WINNERS

1. How many times have Liverpool won the European Super Cup?

2. In which year did the Reds claim their first triumph in the competition?

3. Which West German club did the Reds beat to win their first European Super Cup?

4. Can you recall the name of the striker who scored the Reds' first ever goal in the competition?

5. In which stadium did the Reds lift the 2001 European Super Cup?

EUROPEAN SUPER CUP WINNERS

6. Can you recall Liverpool's 2001 European Super Cup Final opponents?

7. Which team did the Reds beat in the 2005 European Super Cup Final?

8. Name any two of the Reds' three goal scorers in the 2001 European Super Cup Final.

9. Who was the last Red to score a goal in the European Super Cup Final?

10. On how many occasions have the Reds participated in the European Cup Final as winners of the UEFA Cup?

105

REDS IN PRINT

Match the book with
its author:

1.	*Over The Top – My Anfield Secrets*	John Aldridge
2.	*Life at the Kop*	Sami Hyypia
3.	*A Matter of Opinion*	Billy Liddell
4.	*My Story*	Roy Evans
5.	*The Management Years*	Alan Hansen
6.	*Ray of Hope*	Phil Neal
7.	*My Soccer Story*	Graeme Souness
8.	*From Voikkaa to the Premiership*	Michael Owen
9.	*Ghosts on the Wall*	Tommy Smith
10.	*Off the Record*	Ray Kennedy

106

TESTIMONIALS

Match the player with the
team providing the opposition
for his Testimonial match:

1.	Jan Mølby	*Don Revie XI*
2.	Steve Heighway	*Glasgow Celtic*
3.	Bill Shankly	*Newcastle United*
4.	Billy Liddell	*Lancashire XI*
5.	Ian St John	*Borussia Mönchengladbach*
6.	Ian Rush	*PSV Eindhoven*
7.	Ronnie Whelan	*International XI*
8.	Ian Callaghan	*Osasuna*
9.	Sammy Lee	*Everton*
10.	Emlyn Hughes	*Chelsea*

LEAGUE CUP WINNERS (I)

1. Including the 2008/09 competition, how many times have the Reds won the League Cup?

2. In which year did the Reds win the League Cup for the first time in the club's history?

3. Can you recall the year in which Liverpool reached their first League Cup Final?

4. Who was the first Liverpool player to score in a League Cup Final?

5. In which year did the Reds last win the League Cup?

LEAGUE CUP WINNERS (I)

6. Can you recall the 1983 FA Cup
    winners which the Reds beat
    in the 1983 League Cup Final?

7. Who scored the Reds' winner
    in the 1984 League Cup Final
    1–0 win over Everton?

8. In which season during the
    1990s did Liverpool win the
    League Cup?

9. During his illustrious Anfield
    career, which player never won
    a League Cup winners' medal
    with the Reds but the season
    after he left Liverpool he
    captained a cup-winning
    team?

10. In which year did the Reds
    appear in their last League Cup
    Final?

RON YEATS

1. In which Scottish city was Ron born?

2. Prior to signing for the Reds, which Scottish club did Ron play for?

3. In which year did the Reds sign Ron?

4. To the nearest £5,000, how much did the Reds pay to secure the services of Ron?

5. Can you recall the Liverpool manager who brought him to Anfield?

RON YEATS

6. Which club did Ron sign for when he left Anfield?

7. To the nearest 50, how many games did Ron play for the Reds?

8. Can you recall the first trophy Ron won with the Reds?

9. How many goals did Ron score for the Reds – 16, 26 or 36?

10. In which year did Ron leave Anfield?

PLAYERS (IV)

1. Who was the first player Bob Paisley bought when he was appointed the Liverpool manager?

2. When England met Wales at Wembley on 19 May 1971, the entire Liverpool defence played. Name any 3 of the 4 Reds who helped England to a 0–0 draw.

3. Kevin Keegan played his last international for England at the 1982 World Cup Finals in Spain. Which country were England's opponents?

4. How many Scottish Championship winners' medals did Graeme Souness win as a player with Glasgow Rangers?

5. Who scored the only goal of the game when Liverpool ended Chelsea's 86-game unbeaten home run on 26 October 2008?

109

PLAYERS (IV)

6. What injury ended Mark Lawrenson's football playing career?

7. What unique distinction does Peter Crouch hold in terms of the England national team?

8. Who was the tenth Liverpool player to captain England?

9. Name the Liverpool striker who was awarded the Football Writers' Association Footballer of the Year Award in 1979 and in 1983.

10. Which Red is the only player to have scored three consecutive hat-tricks for Liverpool?

MIXED BAG (IV)

1. Which famous words appear above the Shankly Gates?

2. Can you name the only team to have won more European Super Cups than Liverpool?

3. Name the Liverpool player who scored the Reds' first FA Premier League goal of the 2006/07 season.

4. On 14 August 1978, Liverpool visited Glasgow Celtic for a Testimonial match. Who was the game played for?

5. Can you recall the 1973 game which the Reds refused to play?

6. Liverpool played Norwich City at Anfield on 30 April 1994 in what was the last game in front of the old standing Kop. Can you name the last player to score in front of the old Kop?

MIXED BAG (IV)

7. In 2006, Liverpool played Everton in a replay of the 1986 FA Cup Final for Cancer Research. What was the score of the game?

8. Which famous Liverpool manager once said, 'Mind, I've been here during the bad times, too. One year we came second'?

9. Up to and including England's win over Greece in August 2006, only four other clubs have supplied more England internationals than Liverpool. Name any two of the four.

10. Name the Premier League club Liverpool played in season 2008/09 who had two different shirt sponsors during the season.

FOR THE RECORD

1. Prior to Fernando Torres' arrival at Anfield in the summer of 2007, which player held the record for the highest transfer fee paid by Liverpool for a player?

2. Why is Ned Doig's name in the Liverpool record books?

3. Who scored a record 41 League goals for the Reds in season 1961/62?

4. Who holds the Reds' record for the most number of career goals – 346 – scored for the club?

5. Who became the club's oldest goal scorer when he found the net against Stoke City on 5

111

FOR THE RECORD

March 1960, aged 38 years and 55 days?

6. What score is the Reds' record win?

7. In which Cup competition did the Reds set their record win?

8. Which Red has scored the highest number of hat-tricks for Liverpool – 17 from 1926 to 1936?

9. What is the record fee received by the Reds for a player?

10. The record attendance at Anfield is 61,905. Who were the visitors that day?

AWAY DAYS (IV)

1. If Liverpool visited the Hawthorns, which team would they be playing away?

2. If Liverpool visited Loftus Road, which team would they be playing away?

3. If Liverpool visited the Millmoor Ground, which United would they be playing away?

4. If Liverpool visited the McCain Stadium, which team would they be playing away?

5. If Liverpool visited the Boleyn Ground, which team would they be playing away?

112

AWAY DAYS (IV)

6. If Liverpool visited the Madjeski Stadium, which team would they be playing away?

7. If Liverpool visited Glanford Park, which team would they be playing away?

8. If Liverpool visited Spotland, which team would they be playing away?

9. If Liverpool visited Haig Avenue, which team would they be playing away?

10. If Liverpool visited Agborough Stadium, which team would they be playing away?

TOMMY SMITH

1. In which year during the early 1960s did the Reds sign Tommy?

2. After leaving Anfield, which Welsh club did Tommy sign for?

3. To the nearest 50, how many League appearances did Tommy make for Liverpool?

4. In which year did Tommy leave Anfield?

5. How many First Division Championships did Tommy win with the Reds?

113

TOMMY SMITH

6. Tommy missed the 1978 European Cup Final because of an injury. What type of injury did he sustain?

7. Who did Tommy succeed as the captain of Liverpool?

8. In all competitions, how many appearances did Tommy make for Liverpool – 618, 638 or 658?

9. Which trophies were won by the club while Tommy was captain in the 1972/73 season?

10. Which shirt number did Tommy wear when Bill Shankly wanted to confuse the Reds' opponents?

114

KENNY DALGLISH (III)

1. Can you name the former Anfield favourite who Kenny brought to Celtic Park to be the new manager of Glasgow Celtic?

2. During his early years with Glasgow Celtic, Kenny was a key member of their famous youth team that also included future Celtic stars such as Danny McGrain. By what sweet-sounding name was the team known?

3. Name any year in which Kenny received a Championship winners' medal with Celtic.

4. How many times did Kenny win the Scottish Cup?

114

KENNY DALGLISH (III)

5. In which year did he win his only Scottish League Cup winners' medal?

6. How many European Cups did Kenny win?

7. Can you recall any year in which Kenny lifted the European Cup?

8. With which team did Kenny win the Premier League?

9. Who did Kenny replace as the manager of Liverpool?

10. In which season did Kenny become the player-manager of Liverpool?

GRAEME SOUNESS (II)

1.   Name the Italian Serie B club
     Graeme managed in 1997 only
     to be sacked after just six
     League games.

2.   From 1997 to 1999, Graeme
     managed which Portuguese
     club?

3.   Graeme managed which club
     from 2004 to 2006?

4.   From 1971 to 1973, which
     London club did Graeme play
     for?

5.   Which Canadian club did
     Graeme play for in 1972?

6.   How many times did Graeme
     win the European Cup?

115

GRAEME SOUNESS (II)

7. Can you name the legendary Glasgow Rangers manager Graeme succeeded at Ibrox Stadium?

8. How many times did Graeme guide Glasgow Rangers to Scottish League Cup success?

9. Name the England football team deputy captain who was one of the first players Graeme signed for Glasgow Rangers.

10. What was the first trophy Rangers won under Graeme's management?

116

PHIL THOMPSON (II)

1. In which year was Phil appointed the captain of Liverpool?

2. Name the Liverpool manager who appointed Phil as the captain of Liverpool.

3. How many England caps did Phil win – 43, 53 or 63?

4. In his first full season at Anfield, Phil won a First Division Championship winners' medal, a UEFA Cup winners' medal plus one other medal. Can you recall the third medal he won?

5. Name the Liverpool defender whose position Phil took over in the Reds first team.

PHIL THOMPSON (II)

6. How many goals did Phil score for England – 1, 3 or 5?

7. Can you recall the prolific striker that Phil completely man-marked out of the 1974 FA Cup Final?

8. Which England manager awarded Phil his first senior international cap?

9. When Phil made his full England début, four of his Liverpool team-mates were in the starting England XI. Name any two of the four.

10. How many First Division Championship winners' medals did Phil win?

INTERNATIONALS (V)

1. Name any two Liverpool players who played for France, including loan spells.

2. Which player is the only South African international to have played for the Reds?

3. Up to the end of 2007, can you name the two Senegalese internationals to have played for the Reds?

4. What nationality is Sami Hyypia?

5. Which player is the only Polish international to have played for the Reds?

6. Which country did Bruce Grobbelaar play for at international level?

INTERNATIONALS (V)

7. Name any two Liverpool players who played for Norway, including loan spells at Anfield.

8. Which player won eight Welsh caps and scored two goals for his country during his Anfield career?

9. Name either of the players with the surname Parry who played for Liverpool and Wales.

10. Can you name the player whose first name and surname both begin with the same letter who won 18 caps for Wales during his Anfield career?

118

BILL SHANKLY OBE

1. With which Lancashire side did Bill win an FA Cup winners' medal in 1937/38?

2. Which club gave him his first taste of management when they appointed Bill their manager in 1949?

3. Bill once famously said, 'There are only two teams in Liverpool – Liverpool and ...' Who?

4. During the Second World War, Bill played for The Jags. By what name are The Jags better known?

5. In which year was he appointed the manager of the Reds?

118

BILL SHANKLY OBE

6. Which Yorkshire club did he manage immediately before arriving at Anfield?

7. What was the first trophy won by the Reds under Bill?

8. To how many First Division Championships did he guide the Reds?

9. Which Final did he guide the Reds to in 1965/66?

10. Bob Paisley succeeded Bill as the manager of Liverpool but which England World Cup winner did Bill want the Reds to appoint as his successor?

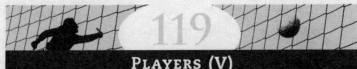

PLAYERS (V)

1. Who is the only England international to have played for Manchester United, Manchester City, Liverpool and Everton?

2. What is Max Thompson's claim to fame in a Liverpool shirt?

3. Against which United did Dirk Kuyt score his first competitive goal for the Reds?

4. Who holds the Reds' record for the most number of League goals – 245 – scored for the club?

5. When Liverpool set their record 11–0 win, which two players failed to get on the score sheet?

6. When this player arrived at Anfield, Bill Shankly told the waiting reporters, 'I've just signed a Colossus. Come in and walk around him'. Who was Bill speaking about?

PLAYERS (V)

7. In which year did Steven Gerrard win the PFA Young Player of the Year Award?

8. Which Red made his final England appearance against Denmark on 21 September 1983?

9. Which Red wasn't on song on 23 August 1999 when he scored an own-goal against Leeds United at Elland Road?

10. Can you name the Red who was the last player to score a goal at Wembley during the last ever competitive football match to be played at the old stadium?

MIXED BAG (V)

1. Which Liverpool legend was the only player to be capped at full international level by England in all three decades of the 1960s, 1970s and 1980s?

2. Liverpool are just one of four clubs to have won the (old) Second Division Championship and the First Division Championship titles in successive seasons. Name any two of the remaining three.

3. Name the Liverpool manager who was in charge of the team for the 1985 European Cup Final.

4. Which club did Liverpool knock out of the 2008/09 UEFA Champions League in the last 32 Round of the competition?

120

MIXED BAG (V)

5. Which player was appointed the Liverpool captain when Graeme Souness left the club?

6. How many European Finals did the Reds reach under the management of Bill Shankly?

7. Which trophy did then Bolton Wanderers manager Phil Neal win at Wembley in 1988/89?

8. Which Liverpool player won the 1984 Professional Football Association's Players' Player of the Year Award?

9. Who was the first Liverpool player to score a hat-trick for England?

10. How many goals did the Reds score in their successful 1976/77 European Cup campaign?

121

BRUCE GROBBELAAR (II)

1. In which year did Bruce join the Reds?

2. Which country did Bruce play for at international level?

3. At which 'space-sounding' South African team did Bruce begin his professional football career?

4. Name either of the other players who were accused along with Bruce of being involved in a match-fixing scandal.

5. Complete the title of Bruce's autobiography – *More Than …*

BRUCE GROBBELAAR (II)

6. Can you name the football team Bruce managed in 1999?

7. Bruce was the player-manager on two occasions of which team?

8. Can you recall the first piece of silverware which Bruce won with the Reds?

9. In 2001, Bruce managed a team named Hellenic, but which country are they from?

10. Can you recall the year in which Bruce left Anfield?

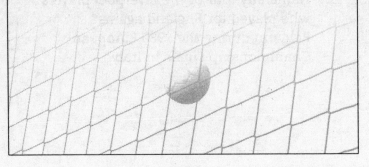

THREE LIONS ON A SHIRT (II)

1. Who was the only Red to be capped by England during the 1930s?

2. Up to and including England's win over Greece in August 2006, only one other club had players who had won more England caps in total than Liverpool players had won. Can you name them?

3. Who was the first Red to be capped by England during the 1960s?

4. How many Liverpool players played for England against Belgium during the 1980 European Championship Finals in Italy?

5. Name any four of the Liverpool players who played for England against Belgium during the 1980 European Championship Finals in Italy.

122

THREE LIONS ON A SHIRT (II)

6. How many Liverpool players played for England against Albania on 5 September 2001?

7. Up to and including England's win over Greece in August 2006, more Liverpool players had appeared as a substitute for England than any other club. To the nearest 20, how many had appeared?

8. Name any four of the Liverpool players who started for England against Switzerland on 7 September 1977.

9. What unique distinction does former Red Paul Ince, then of Manchester United, hold in terms of the England captaincy?

10. Which former Red was England manager Ron Greenwood's preferred choice as captain and would have led England at the 1982 World Cup Finals had he been fit?

123

ALAN HANSEN

1. Prior to signing for Liverpool, which Scottish club did Alan play for?

2. To the nearest 50, how many League appearances did Alan make for the Reds?

3. In which year did Alan sign for Liverpool?

4. To the nearest 10, how many League goals did Alan score for the Reds?

5. In which year did Alan leave Anfield?

ALAN HANSEN

6. Where can Alan normally be found on a Saturday in homes throughout the United Kingdom?

7. How old was Alan when he made his League début for Liverpool – 20, 22 or 24?

8. To the nearest £10,000, how much did Liverpool pay for Alan's services?

9. How many full international caps did Alan win – 26, 36 or 46?

10. Against which former First Division Champions from the 1970s did Alan make his début for the Reds?

EUROPEAN CUP WINNERS 1980/81

1. Which team did Liverpool beat in the 1981 European Cup Final?

2. The Reds played which Finnish club in the first round?

3. Which city hosted the 1980/81 European Cup Final?

4. Can you recall the Reds' biggest home win in the 1980/81 competition?

5. Name the German side the Reds beat in the semi-final.

6. Can you recall the Bulgarian side Liverpool beat en route to lifting the European Cup in 1980/81?

124

EUROPEAN CUP WINNERS 1980/81

7. How many of their nine games in the 1980/81 competition did the Reds lose?

8. Who scored two hat-tricks in the Reds' successful 1980/81 European Cup campaign and was their joint top goal scorer in the competition with Terry McDermott on six goals each?

9. Who scored the all-important goal in a 1–1 semi-final away draw that put Liverpool through to the 1980/81 European Cup Final thanks to an aggregate score of 2–1?

10. The Reds won the 1980/81 European Cup Final 1–0 but can you recall who scored the all-important goal?

125

ROGER HUNT

1. What was the first trophy Roger won with Liverpool?

2. In which year did the Reds sign Roger?

3. To the nearest 50, how many first-team appearances did Roger make for Liverpool?

4. How many international games did Roger play for England during his Anfield career – 30, 32 or 34?

5. To the nearest 30, how many goals did Roger score for Liverpool?

125

ROGER HUNT

6. In which year did Roger receive an MBE?

7. What affectionate nickname did Liverpool fans commonly use to refer to Roger?

8. After leaving Anfield, which club did Roger sign for?

9. Can you recall the Second Division United which Roger scored against when he made his Liverpool début on 9 September 1959?

10. In which year did Roger leave Anfield?

LIVERPOOL'S CUP TREBLE (I)

1. In which season did Liverpool win their Cup Treble?

2. Which team did Liverpool beat in the FA Cup Final in the year they won their Treble?

3. The Reds beat which United in the UEFA Cup semi-final?

4. Can you recall the Reds' goal scorer in the League Cup Final the year they won their Treble?

5. Who scored for the Reds in both legs of their League Cup semi-final?

6. Can you recall the Romanian side the Reds beat on their way to winning one of the three Cups?

126

LIVERPOOL'S CUP TREBLE (I)

7. Liverpool lost 1–0 to which City in a pre-season friendly before the beginning of their successful Treble-winning season, as well as beating the same City 8–0 in Round 4 of the League Cup?

8. Can you name the Reds' leading goal scorer in their successful FA Cup campaign in the year they won their Treble?

9. Name any Red who scored in the UEFA Cup Final in the year they won their Treble.

10. Where was Liverpool's FA Cup semi-final played in the year they won their Treble?

127

FA CUP WINNERS 1991/92

1. Which team did the Reds beat at Wembley in 1991/92 to lift the FA Cup?

2. Liverpool beat which team with an 'x' in their name in Round 3?

3. Who scored the Reds' winning goal in a 1–0 FA Cup sixth-round victory over Aston Villa?

4. Can you recall the score in the Final?

5. At which club's stadium did the Reds draw 1–1 with Portsmouth in their FA Cup semi-final tie?

FA CUP WINNERS 1991/92

6. Can you name the manager who guided the Reds to FA Cup glory in 1991/92?

7. The Reds defeated the 1980/81 UEFA Cup Winners in Round 5. Can you name them?

8. Who scored home and away for the Reds against Bristol Rovers in Round 4?

9. Apart from John Barnes, who else scored three goals for the Reds during their successful 1991/92 FA Cup campaign?

10. Name both of Liverpool's goal scorers in the 1991/92 Final.

128

LEAGUE CHAMPIONS 1989/90

1. How many points did the Reds end the season with?

2. The Reds beat which Lancashire rivals 3–1 at Anfield on the opening day of the season?

3. Against which former First Division Champions from the 1970s did the Reds record their first League away win of the season?

4. Can you name the Liverpool player who scored both goals for the Reds in a 2–1 away win over Manchester United?

5. How many of their 19 League home games did Liverpool win?

LEAGUE CHAMPIONS 1989/90

6. Who finished the season as the Reds' top League goal scorer with 22 goals?

7. Liverpool won 6–1 away on the last day of the League season to wrap up their campaign in style. Can you name their opponents?

8. Can you name the former European Cup winners with whom the Reds drew 2–2 away on New Year's Day?

9. What was the score when the Reds beat Crystal Palace at Anfield on 12 September 1989?

10. The Reds beat which London side 1–0 at home and 2–1 away?

THE CHAMPIONS

1. In which decade did the Reds clinch their first ever English First Division Championship?

2. How many times did the Reds win the English First Division Championship during the 1980s?

3. Can you name the Reds manager who won more English First Division titles than any other manager in the history of the club?

4. In which season during the 1960s did the Reds clinch their first English First Division Championship of the decade?

5. How many times did the Reds win the English Second Division Championship?

6. Can you recall the season in which the Reds won their first English League

129

THE CHAMPIONS

Division One Championship post-
World War II?

7. Name the seasons in which the Reds
won back-to-back English Second
Division and English First Division
Championships.

8. Which Liverpool manager who guided
the Reds to their inaugural English First
Division Championship also shares the
same name as an American golfer who
won the British Open Championship
five times?

9. How many different managers guided
the Reds to the English First Division
Championship during the 1980s?

10. Name any two seasons in which the
Reds won the English Second Division
Championship.

CUP MIXTURE

1. Can you name the reigning First Division Champions who put Liverpool out of the 1975/76 FA Cup in Round 4 of the competition?

2. Which dynamic midfielder scored the Reds' 50th goal in the European Cup during the 1976/77 competition?

3. How many FA Cup Finals did the Reds win at the Millennium Stadium?

4. Name the Wanderers that Liverpool beat en route to winning the FA Cup in 1965.

5. Name any future Liverpool player who played for Newcastle United against the Reds in the 1974 FA Cup Final.

130

CUP MIXTURE

6. In which round did the Reds exit the 1976/77 League Cup?

7. Name the Spanish side the Reds beat in Round 4 of their successful 1975/76 UEFA Cup campaign.

8. What was the score of the game when Liverpool beat Luton Town at Kenilworth Road in Round 3 of their successful 2005/06 FA Cup-winning campaign?

9. How many FA Cup Finals did the Reds win under Bill Shankly?

10. Name the team that put the Reds out of the FA Cup in Round 3 in January 2007.

131

Mixed Bag (VI)

1. In which year did Bill Shankly step down as the Liverpool manager?

2. Which future Red won the 1999 PFA Young Player of the Year Award?

3. Name the player who has won more England caps at full-back than Phil Neal?

4. Which United did Mark Lawrenson once manage?

5. Which Martin scored an own-goal playing for West Ham United against the Reds at Anfield on 6 November 1993?

MIXED BAG (VI)

6. In which season did Bob Paisley guide Liverpool to their first ever League Cup Final win?

7. At which stadium did the Reds draw with Leicester City in the 1974 FA Cup semi-final?

8. Which Willie scored a penalty for the Reds in their 1965 FA Cup semi-final?

9. Who was the Reds' leading goal scorer in their successful 1975/76 UEFA Cup campaign?

10. Up to and including the 2006 FA Community Shield, how many times have the Reds played at the Millennium Stadium?

LEAGUE CHAMPIONS 1987/88

1. To the nearest five, how many points did the Reds end the season with?

2. The Reds beat the following season's League Champions 2–1 away on the opening day of the season. Name them.

3. The Reds only lost two League games all season. Name either of the victors.

4. Can you name the Town the Reds drew 1–1 with on the final day of the league season?

5. How many League home games did the Reds play?

132

LEAGUE CHAMPIONS 1987/88

6. Who finished the season as the Reds' top League goal scorer with 26 goals?

7. Liverpool won 3–0 away at this United on Boxing Day. Can you name their opponents?

8. The Reds beat the 1987/88 FA Cup winners 2–1 at Anfield on 26 March 1988. Can you name the FA Cup winners who spoilt Liverpool's Double dream?

9. What was the Reds' biggest League win of the season?

10. In how many of their League games did the Reds fail to score?

FA CUP WINNERS 1988/89

1. Which team did the Reds beat at Wembley in the 1989 FA Cup Final?

2. In Round 3, the Reds beat a team which at one time were managed by the legendary Bill Shankly. Can you name them?

3. Which team did Liverpool beat in the semi-finals?

4. Can you recall the score in the Final?

5. Who scored for the Reds in both the semi-final and in the Final?

133

FA CUP WINNERS 1988/89

6. Can you name the manager
    who guided the Reds to FA Cup
    glory in 1988/89?

7. The Reds defeated which City
    in Round 5?

8. At which stadium did the Reds
    win their semi-final tie?

9. Which club did the Reds beat
    4–0 at Anfield in Round 6?

10. Who, with six goals, was the
    Reds' top goal scorer in their
    successful 1988/89 FA Cup-
    winning campaign?

LIVERPOOL'S CUP TREBLE (II)

1. Which team did Liverpool beat in the 2001 UEFA Cup Final?

2. Who scored both of Liverpool's goals in the 2001 FA Cup Final?

3. The Reds beat which United in the FA Cup third round?

4. Which team did Liverpool beat in the League Cup Final?

5. Can you recall the Italian side the Reds beat on their way to winning the 2001 UEFA Cup?

6. Name the team the Reds defeated in the 2001 FA Cup semi-final.

134

LIVERPOOL'S CUP TREBLE (II)

7. In which club's stadium did Liverpool win the 2001 UEFA Cup Final?

8. Apart from Michael Owen, who else scored four goals for the Reds in their successful 2000/01 UEFA Cup campaign?

9. Liverpool lost one game during their successful 2000/01 League Cup campaign. Can you recall the team who beat them in the first leg of the semi-final?

10. In total, how many games did the Reds play in the FA Cup, League Cup and the UEFA Cup?

LEAGUE CUP WINNERS (II)

1. At which ground did the Reds lose their first League Cup Final appearance?

2. Which team did the Reds lose to in the 1978 League Cup Final?

3. Can you recall the team Liverpool beat to clinch their first League Cup Final success?

4. In which year did the Reds win their fourth consecutive League Cup Final?

5. At which stadium did the Reds achieve their first League Cup Final victory?

LEAGUE CUP WINNERS (II)

6. Can you recall the 1982 FA Cup winners which the Reds beat in the 1982 League Cup Final?

7. Which team did the Reds beat in the 1995 League Cup Final?

8. Liverpool lost the 2005 League Cup Final 3–2 to which team?

9. The League Cup was the only trophy won by which manager during his time in charge of the team?

10. At which ground did the Reds beat Everton in the 1984 League Cup Final replay?

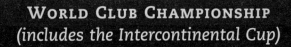

WORLD CLUB CHAMPIONSHIP
(includes the Intercontinental Cup)

1. How many times have the Reds been crowned World Club Champions (including the Intercontinental Cup)?

2. In how many World Club Championship Finals have the Reds appeared?

3. In which year did the Reds first participate in the World Club Championship Final?

4. Name the first team the Reds played in the World Club Championship Final.

5. In which City did the Reds compete in their first World Club Championship Final?

6. How many goals in total have the Reds scored in the World

WORLD CLUB CHAMPIONSHIP
(includes the Intercontinental Cup)

Club Championship Final (the Final only)?

7. Liverpool declined to play Boca Juniors in the 1977 World Club Championship Final. Which European team replaced them in the Final?

8. Why did the Reds not participate in the 1978 World Club Championship Final?

9. Can you name the South American team which Liverpool were scheduled to play in the 1978 World Club Championship Final?

10. Which Brazilian team beat Liverpool 1–0 in the 2005 World Club Championship Final?

LEAGUE CHAMPIONS 1972/73

1. To the nearest five, how many points did the Reds end the season with?

2. The Reds beat which Lancashire opponents 2–0 at Anfield on the opening day of the season?

3. Against which United did the Reds record their biggest League win of the season?

4. When the Reds suffered their last League defeat of the 1972/73 season, a 2–1 reversal on 21 April 1973, Kevin Keegan scored against which club he would later play for?

5. On 10 February 1972, the Reds lost their only home League game of the season to which London club?

6.   Who finished the season as the Reds' top League goal scorer with 13 goals?

7.   Liverpool drew 0–0 with which City on the last day of the 1972/73 League season?

8.   Can you name the United against which the Reds recorded their first win of 1973?

9.   Which industrious player scored the Reds' first League goal of the season?

10. Which Red scored in four consecutive League games between 23 August 1972 and 2 September 1972?

DOUBLE WINNERS 1985/86 (II)

1. Which manager guided
    Liverpool to Double success in
    1985/86?

2. Name the club which was the
    last team the Reds lost to in
    the League in season 1985/86.

3. In the 1985/86 FA Cup semi-
    finals, the Reds disposed of
    the 1975/76 FA Cup winners
    after extra-time. Which club
    did they squeeze past?

4. How many of their 21 League
    home games did Liverpool win?

5. Which player scored two
    penalties during Liverpool's
    successful 1985/86 FA Cup
    campaign?

DOUBLE WINNERS 1985/86 (II)

6. Who finished the season as the Reds' top League goal scorer with 22 goals?

7. Can you recall the City that the Reds beat 5–0 at Anfield in Round 3 of the 1985/86 FA Cup?

8. The Reds needed a replay to see off which lowly City in Round 5?

9. How many of their 42 League games did the Reds lose in season 1985/86?

10. Which player scored the Reds' last League goal of the season?

AWARDS (II)

1. Name the Liverpool manager who was awarded the PFA Merit Award in 1983.

2. Who is the only Liverpool player to have won the coveted BBC Sports Personality of the Year Award?

3. Name the Liverpool striker who was awarded the Football Writers' Association Footballer of the Year Award in 1984.

4. Who, in 1987, became only the second recipient from Liverpool FC of the Football Writers' Tribute Award?

5. In 1988, who became the last Red to win the Professional Football Association's Players' Player of the Year Award?

AWARDS (II)

6. Which future Red, then at Luton Town, won the 1984 PFA Young Player of the Year Award?

7. Which former Red, and England international, won the 1982 Professional Football Association's Players' Player of the Year Award?

8. Name any two of the four Reds who were among the first 29 inductees of the National Football Museum when it was opened on 1 December 2002.

9. Who was the first Red to win the Professional Football Association's Players' Player of the Year Award?

10. In which year did Michael Owen win the PFA Young Player of the Year Award?

140

THE WELSH CONNECTION

1. On how many occasions have the Reds meet Wrexham in a Football League game – 0, 2 or 4?

2. Remarkably, which Welsh side have beaten Liverpool in their last five League meetings between the two sides?

3. The Reds have met Swansea four times in the FA Cup. How many of these games did Liverpool win?

4. The Reds beat which Welsh side in both the 1962/63 and 1969/70 FA Cup?

5. With which legendary England centre forward does Ian Rush share the record for the most League Cup goals – 49?

140

THE WELSH CONNECTION

6. Against which former World Cup winners did Dean Saunders score a memorable goal for Wales giving them a famous 1–0 win in Cardiff in 1991?

7. Kenny Dalglish scored a hat-trick against which Welsh side in the 1977/78 League Cup competition?

8. Ian Rush is the record FA Cup goal scorer with 44 goals. How many of those were during the time he spent at Anfield?

9. The Reds have met Cardiff City twice in the FA Cup. How many times did the Reds win?

10. Ian Rush has scored more goals in the FA Cup Final than any other player. How many times did he score?

UEFA CHAMPIONS LEAGUE GLORY
2004/05

1. Which Austrian side did Liverpool beat in the 3rd qualifying round of the competition?

2. Name the French team which was in Liverpool's group.

3. Which Greek side was the first team to beat Liverpool in the 2004/05 UEFA Champions League competition?

4. Which Spanish team did Liverpool beat away and draw with at home? (They also finished last in group A.)

5. Liverpool beat which German Bundesliga side 6–2 on aggregate in the first knockout stage?

141

UEFA CHAMPIONS LEAGUE GLORY
2004/05

6. Name either of Liverpool's goal scorers when they beat Juventus 2–1 at Anfield in the first leg of their quarter-final tie.

7. In which city was the 2005 UEFA Champions League Final played?

8. Can you recall the name of Liverpool's semi-final opponents?

9. Liverpool drew 3–3 with AC Milan in the Final. Name any two of Liverpool's three goal scorers in the Final.

10. Who was the only Liverpool player to miss in the penalty shootout?

JOE FAGAN

1. Who did Joe succeed as the manager of Liverpool?

2. In which season did Joe take charge at Anfield?

3. Where in England was Joe born?

4. Joe began his managerial career at which naval-sounding Lancashire Combination League team which he led to two Championships in 1949/50 and 1951/52?

5. In which year during the late 1950s did Joe arrive at Anfield as a trainer?

142

JOE FAGAN

6. What was the first trophy the Reds won under Joe's management?

7. In his first full season in charge of the Reds, which Cup(s) did Liverpool win?

8. How many times did the Reds secure the First Division Championship under Joe's management?

9. Joe won promotion to the English First Division as a player with which Lancashire club in 1946/47?

10. At the end of which season did Joe step down as Liverpool manager?

143

THE PREMIERSHIP YEARS (II)

1. What was of historic significance about the Merseyside derby played at Goodison Park on 11 December 2004 which Everton won 1–0?

2. Eight players have scored in the Premiership for five different clubs, two of them for Liverpool. Name the two Reds and any two other clubs they scored a Premier League goal for.

3. Can you name the player who on 29 October 2000 ran out at Anfield to cries of 'Judas' from the Everton fans?

THE PREMIERSHIP YEARS (II)

4. Liverpool have played two teams in the Premier League whose name begins and ends with the same letter. Name both teams.

5. During the 2001/02 season, Everton announced plans to move away from their Goodison Park home and relocate to a brand-new 55,000 all-seater stadium on the banks of the River Mersey. Radio phone-ins were busy with both sets of fans objecting to a ground share with one Evertonian claiming he wouldn't share a particular chocolate bar with a Liverpool fan, never mind a football stadium. Name the chocolate bar.

THE PREMIERSHIP YEARS (II)

6. Since the inception of the Premier League in season 1992/93, Liverpool is one of only seven teams to have played every season of the League's history, including season 2008/09. Name any five of the other six.

7. Which club presented Liverpool fans with the longest journey for an away game in the 2008/09 Premier League season?

8. On 22 October 2007, the Professional Game Match Board announced that this referee would not be refereeing a Premier League match over the weekend of 27–28 October 2007 following severe criticism concerning his handling of the 206th Merseyside derby three days earlier at Goodison Park. Name the referee.

THE PREMIERSHIP YEARS (II)

9. At the start of the 2007/08 Premier League season, a total of 330 foreign players were registered as first-team players with the 20 Premiership clubs. Of these teams only one of them had fewer English players in their squad than Liverpool (4). Name the team.

10. Liverpool have played eight Premier League teams in an away game where the home side has played the Reds at two different grounds. Name any five of the eight, including the grounds they played at.

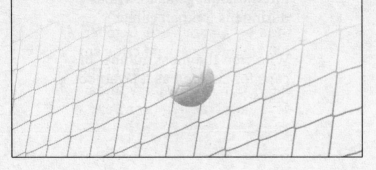

INTERNATIONALS (VI)

1. Can you name the player whose first name and surname both begin with the same letter who scored seven goals for his country during his Anfield career?

2. Which player won 37 caps for Scotland during his time with the Reds?

3. Who was the first Danish international to play for the Reds?

4. Name the former Liverpool player who scored 14 international goals for Wales during his football career.

5. Who won the most number of caps for England as a Liverpool player?

144

INTERNATIONALS (VI)

6. How many goals did Terry McDermott score for England during his Anfield career?

7. Name any of the three Liverpool players who played in a war-time international for Wales during their Anfield career.

8. Tom Miller scored two international goals for Scotland as a Liverpool player. How many international caps did he win during his Anfield career?

9. Can you name the only Liverpool player to have played for a Great Britain international select side?

10. Which country did Rigobert Song play for at international level?

145

GRAEME SOUNESS (III)

1. To the nearest 10, how many full international caps did Graeme win with Scotland?

2. Against which European country, which no longer exists, did Graeme make his international début?

3. Graeme left Glasgow Rangers to become the manager of which club?

4. How many English First Division Championships did Graeme win with Liverpool?

5. In which City was Graeme born?

GRAEME SOUNESS (III)

6.   Glasgow Rangers won three
     Scottish League Cups under
     his management. Which team
     did they beat in two of the
     Finals?

7.   How many English League
     Cups did Graeme win with
     Liverpool?

8.   Graeme won 54 international
     caps with Scotland. How many
     of them did he win as a player
     with Rangers – 2, 3 or 4?

9.   Name the former English FA
     Premier League winners of
     which Graeme was appointed
     the manager in March 2000.

10. Who did Graeme succeed as
     the manager of Newcastle
     United?

FA CUP WINNERS 2005/06

1. Which team did the Reds beat at the Millennium Stadium in 2005/06 to lift the FA Cup?

2. Liverpool beat which club in Round 4?

3. What was so unusual about Xabi Alonso's goal against Luton Town in Round 3?

4. Can you recall the score in the Final at the end of normal time?

5. Which FA Premier League club did Liverpool beat in the semi-finals?

146

FA CUP WINNERS 2005/06

6. Who scored the Reds' first goal of their successful 2005/06 FA Cup campaign?

7. Can you recall the City Liverpool disposed of in the quarter-finals?

8. Name any two Liverpool players who scored in the penalty shoot-out.

9. Can you name the team the Reds beat in Round 5?

10. Which stadium hosted Liverpool's 2005/06 FA Cup semi-final?

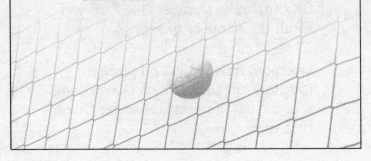

CHRISTMAS NUMBER ONES (III)

1. Liverpool won Division 1 in 1980 and
    John Lennon had the UK Christmas
    Number One. Can you recall the name
    of the song?

2. Liverpool finished in 6th place in the
    FA Premier League in 1993. Which
    group had the UK Christmas Number
    One hit that year with 'Babe'?

3. Liverpool won Division 1 and Slade
    had the UK Christmas Number One
    the same year with 'Merry Xmas
    Everybody'. What was the year?

4. Liverpool finished in 3rd place in the
    FA Premier League in 2001 and Robbie
    Williams and Nicole Kidman had the
    UK Christmas Number One. Can you
    recall the name of the song?

5. Liverpool finished in 2nd place in
    Division 1 in 1975. Which Queen song
    was the UK Christmas Number One hit
    that year?

CHRISTMAS NUMBER ONES (III)

6.   Liverpool won Division 1 and Cliff Richard had the UK Christmas Number One the same year with 'Mistletoe and Wine'. What was the year?

7.   Liverpool finished in 6th place in Division 1 in 1992 and Whitney Houston had the UK Christmas Number One with which song?

8.   Liverpool finished in 3rd place in the FA Premier League in 1996. Which group had the UK Christmas Number One with 'Knockin' On Heaven's Door'.

9.   Liverpool won Division 1 and Johnny Mathis had the UK Christmas Number One the same year with 'When A Child Is Born'. What was the year?

10. Liverpool finished in 2nd place in Division 1 in 1978. Which group had the UK Christmas Number One hit that year with 'Mary's Boy Child'?

WHO ARE WE PLAYING? (V)

1. If Liverpool were in opposition against the Red Devils, who would they be playing?

2. If Liverpool were in opposition against the Hatters, which Town would they be playing?

3. If Liverpool were in opposition against the Grecians, which City would they be playing?

4. If Liverpool were in opposition against the 'O's, who would they be playing?

5. If Liverpool were in opposition against the Grays, which Athletic would they be playing?

WHO ARE WE PLAYING? (V)

6. If Liverpool were in opposition against Pompey, who would they be playing?

7. If Liverpool were in opposition against the Lions, who would they be playing?

8. If Liverpool were in opposition against the MK Dons, who would they be playing?

9. If Liverpool were in opposition against the Cobblers, who would they be playing?

10. If Liverpool were in opposition against the Shaymen, which Town would they be playing?

THE MERSEYSIDE DERBY (VI)

1. What distinction does the city of Liverpool have thanks to Liverpool FC and Everton FC that no other English city can boast?

2. Liverpool is one of only eight cities in England that can claim a local derby (Everton and Liverpool). Can you name five of the remaining seven?

3. Can you name the Liverpool midfielder/forward from the late 1980s who once claimed in a match-day programme interview that, if he could be invisible for a day, he would stand at a pelican crossing all day pressing the button?

4. This midfielder started his career at Everton, the club he supported as a boy, and made his début for the Toffees on 16 August 1980 as a teenager after serving as a ball boy at Goodison Park. He later joined Liverpool. Who is he?

149

THE MERSEYSIDE DERBY (VI)

5. Which Everton striker ended the 1931/32 season with 44 goals including a hat-trick in the Merseyside derby?

6. Which Liverpool striker who had two spells at Anfield (the first from 1992 to 2001) supported Everton as a boy?

7. In 1985/86, Everton was the last team Liverpool lost to on their way to winning the title. What was the score of the game on 22 February 1986?

8. On 13 March 1994, Everton lost the last Merseyside derby at Anfield before the standing Kop was changed to an all-seater stand. Which Everton defender scored Everton's goal that day?

9. In which year did Peter Beardsley make his England début – 1984, 1985 or 1986?

10. In 2006, Everton played Liverpool in a rematch of the 1986 FA Cup Final for Cancer Research. What was the score?

KENNY DALGLISH (IV)

1. In which year did Kenny Dalglish resign as the manager of Liverpool?

2. In which year was Kenny Dalglish appointed Director of Football Operations at Glasgow Celtic?

3. How many times was Kenny voted the English Footballer of the Year?

4. In which year was Kenny voted the English Players' Player of the Year?

5. In which season was he appointed Glasgow Celtic captain?

KENNY DALGLISH (IV)

6. Against which European country did Kenny Dalglish make his international début for Scotland?

7. Who appointed Kenny Dalglish the captain of the Scotland national team in 1978?

8. Who replaced Kenny Dalglish as the captain of Scotland after just four games as captain?

9. In which year did Kenny Dalglish lead Newcastle United to the FA Cup Final?

10. Which club did he manage briefly in 2000?

ANSWERS

1
Trophies
1. 18
2. 4
3. 7
4. 7
5. 10
6. 5
7. 3
8. 3
9. Screen Sport Super Cup
10. The Carlsberg Trophy

2
John Aldridge
1. Oxford United
2. 1987
3. 83
4. Newport County
5. 1989
6. Real Sociedad
7. Tranmere Rovers
8. 50
9. Ireland
10. Aston Villa

3
FA Cup 1976/77
1. Manchester United
2. Bob Paisley
3. Jimmy Case

4. Crystal Palace
5. Kevin Keegan
6. Everton
7. Oldham Athletic
8. Middlesbrough
9. 17
10. Maine Road

4
Kenny Dalglish (I)
1. Glasgow (Dalmarnock on 4 March 1951)
2. 1977
3. 355
4. Liverpool
5. Bob Paisley
6. 3
7. Glasgow Celtic
8. Steve Archibald
9. Holland
10. Liverpool and West Ham United

5
Internationals (I)
1. Ray Clemence
2. Sander Westerveld
3. Hungary
4. Billy Liddell
5. Mark Gonzalez
6. Roger Hunt (1966) and

Dietmar Hamann (2002)

7. Morocco
8. Matt Busby, Willie Fagan, Jim Harley and Billy Liddell (all during WWII)
9. Deportivo de La Coruña
10. Avi Cohen and Ronny Rosenthal

6
The Merseyside Derby (I)

1. 1894
2. 14
3. 5 (between 1932/33 and 1936/37)
4. 1935/36
5. 10
6. Once
7. Neville Southall
8. 6 (includes the 2008/09 FA Cup fourth round tie)
9. 1999/2000 (1–0)
10. 42

7
The Premiership Years (I)

1. Arsenal, Aston Villa, Blackburn Rovers, Chelsea, Coventry City, Crystal Palace, Everton, Ipswich Town, Leeds United, Manchester City, Manchester United, Middlesbrough, Norwich City, Nottingham Forest, Oldham Athletic, Queens Park Rangers, Sheffield United, Sheffield Wednesday, Southampton, Tottenham Hotspur and

Wimbledon
2. Manchester United
3. Jürgen Klinsmann
4. Newcastle United
5. 41
6. Nottingham Forest
7. Arsenal, Chelsea, Everton, Manchester United, Newcastle United, Tottenham Hotspur and West Ham United
8. A club mascot
9. West Bromwich Albion
10. Nick Barmby

8
History

1. 1892
2. Everton
3. 1965
4. West Ham United
5. Wolverhampton Wanderers
6. 1977
7. John Houlding
8. FA Cup, League Cup and UEFA Cup
9. John McKenna and William Barday
10. Bill Shankly

9
Alan Kennedy

1. Sunderland
2. Newcastle United
3. 1978
4. Manchester City (in the 1976 League Cup Final; Liverpool beat them in

the 1974 FA Cup Final)
5. Phil Boersma and
   Graeme Souness
6. Queens Park Rangers
7. The First Division
   Championship in season
   1978/79
8. Barney Rubble
9. Kenny Dalglish (1985)
10. Sunderland

10
This Is Anfield
1. 1884
2. Walton Breck Road
3. The Kemlyn Road Stand
4. 2003 (In January 2004,
   shortly before a Liverpool
   home game, an error
   with the electronic
   scoreboard caused it to
   read: 'LIVERPOOL 54 – 0
   EVERTON')
5. Shankly Gates
6. It swayed
7. SS *Great Eastern*
8. 4
9. Uruguay (prior to this
   England beat Paraguay
   4–0 on 17 April 2002)
10. Stanley Park Stadium

11
Peter Beardsley
1. 1987
2. Newcastle United
3. By bicycle
4. Everton
5. Howard Kendall
6. 46

7. Arsenal
8. £1.9m
9. Wallsend Boys' Club
10. Manchester United

12
Ian Rush
1. Chester City
2. Juventus
3. Ipswich Town (1980/81
   UEFA Cup winners)
4. 469
5. The European Cup
   (versus Oulun Palloseura
   at Anfield)
6. 1996
7. Sheffield United
8. Chester City
9. Wrexham
10. 346

13
League Champions 1976/77
1. 57
2. Norwich City
3. Birmingham City
4. Stoke City
5. 18
6. Kevin Keegan
7. Bristol City
8. Sunderland (2–0 at
   Anfield)
9. David Johnson
10. None

14
Xabi Alonso
1. Spanish
2. Real Sociedad

3. Winning Euro 2008 with Spain
4. Bolton Wanderers
5. Eibar
6. £10.5m
7. 2004
8. FC Barcelona
9. Rafa Benítez
10. Ecuador

15
Internationals (II)
1. Michael Owen
2. Eph Longworth (WWI) and Jack Balmer (WWII)
3. Stéphane Henchoz
4. Michael Owen
5. Fabio Aurelio
6. Kenny Dalglish
7. Ian Rush
8. 1
9. Alou Diarra
10. Billy Lacey (2)

16
Kevin Keegan
1. Scunthorpe United
2. Fulham
3. Germany
4. Newcastle United
5. Hamburger Sport-Verein e. V.
6. Southampton
7. Newcastle United
8. 1999
9. Manchester City
10. 68

17
Reds at the World Cup (I)
1. 1950 (Laurie Hughes for England)
2. Alan Hansen
3. 3
4. Tommy Younger (for Scotland in 1958)
5. 5
6. Roger Hunt (for England in 1966)
7. Stig Inge Bjørnebye (Norway)
8. 0
9. Scotland (3)
10. Michael Owen (England)

18
European Championship Reds (I)
1. 0
2. Roger Hunt (for England in 1968)
3. Phil Thompson (3)
4. Ray Clemence
5. 2 (Ray Houghton and Ronnie Whelan for the Republic of Ireland)
6. Peter Beardsley
7. Steve McManaman (England)
8. 9
9. Steven Gerrard, Emile Heskey and Michael Owen
10. Milan Baros (5 goals for Czech Republic)

19
The Merseyside Derby (II)

1. They were presented with a papier mâché trophy to parade at Anfield
2. 1987/88 (2 First Division games, 1 FA Cup game and 1 League Cup game)
3. Sandy Young
4. Dick Forshaw (with Liverpool in 1922 and 1923 and with Everton in 1928)
5. Robbie Fowler (sent off with David Unsworth at Goodison Park on 16 April 1997)
6. Ian Rush (Liverpool) and Stuart McCall (Everton)
7. Andrew Hannah and Steve McMahon
8. Wayne Clarke
9. Jamie Carragher (21)
10. Fernando Torres

20
Michael Owen

1. 1996
2. 216
3. Real Madrid
4. 2004
5. 17
6. 118
7. Newcastle United
8. Manchester United
9. UEFA Cup and European Super Cup
10. The European Footballer of the Year Award

21
FA Cup Winners 1964/65

1. Leeds United
2. West Bromwich Albion
3. Roger Hunt
4. Liverpool 2 Leeds United 1
5. Chelsea
6. Bill Shankly
7. Leicester City
8. 2
9. Stockport County
10. Roger Hunt and Ian St John

22
Ian Callaghan

1. Billy Liddell
2. Bristol Rovers
3. The Second Division Championship in season 1961/62
4. Gerry Byrne and Roger Hunt
5. The Football Writers' Association Player of the Year
6. Queens Park Rangers
7. Cally
8. Nottingham Forest (1–0 at Old Trafford)
9. John Toshack (manager of Swansea City)
10. Crewe Alexandra

23
Away Days (I)

1. Manchester City
2. Leicester City
3. Hartlepool United

4. Lincoln City
5. Gravesend & Northfleet
6. Sunderland
7. Luton Town
8. Huddersfield Town
9. Macclesfield Town
10. Halifax Town

24
The Reds' First Season in Europe

1. 1964/65
2. The European Cup
3. Reykjavik
4. Gordon Wallace
5. Inter Milan
6. RSC Anderlecht
7. 20
8. The referee tossed a coloured disc and Liverpool called correctly
9. Roger Hunt
10. Ian Callaghan, Roger Hunt and Ian St John

25
Jan Mølby

1. Kolding
2. 218
3. Amsterdamsche Football Club Ajax (Ajax Amsterdam)
4. 1984
5. Barnsley FC
6. 44
7. 1996
8. £575,000
9. Norwich City
10. Swansea City

26
Season 1976/77

1. 4
2. Steve Heighway
3. Phil Neal (pen) and John Toshack
4. Southampton
5. Kevin Keegan
6. Bobby Charlton (Bobby Charlton XI)
7. West Bromwich Albion
8. Phil Neal
9. Jimmy Case
10. 9

27
The Sporting Year (I)

1. 1963
2. 1995
3. 1987
4. 1977
5. 1965
6. 1968
7. 1970
8. 1954
9. 1986
10. 1984

28
Landmark Premiership Goals

1. Mark Walters
2. Emile Heskey
3. Coventry City
4. Manchester United
5. Robbie Fowler
6. Stan Collymore
7. Blackburn Rovers
8. West Bromwich Albion

9. Dietmar Hamann
(v Newcastle United on 2
September 2002)
10. Leeds United

29
The Merseyside Derby (III)

1. Dixie Dean
2. 7 (consecutive victories
at Anfield between
1908/09 and 1914/15)
3. 78,299
4. 1948 (September)
5. A chain of blue and red
club scarves
6. Four
7. Kenny Dalglish resigned
as the manager of
Liverpool
8. 14 games (between the
1970/71 season and
1984/85 season)
9. 15 (between 1899 and
1920 which included 10
victories)
10. 1

30
**European Cup Winners
1976/77**

1. Borussia
Mönchengladbach
2. Crusaders
3. Rome
4. 7–0 (Crusaders 2–0
and 5–0)
5. FC Zurich
6. St Etienne (quarter-
finals)
7. Turkey

8. Terry McDermott,
Tommy Smith and Phil
Neal
9. David Fairclough
10. Kevin Keegan and Phil
Neal

31
**Premiership Own-Goals
and Howlers**

1. Oldham Athletic (16
October 1993 at Anfield)
2. Steve Nicol
(v Middlesbrough away
on 13 March 1993)
3. Neil 'Razor' Ruddock (v
Spurs on 26 October
1994)
4. David Burrows
5. Claus Thomsen
6. Rio Ferdinand
7. Jamie Carragher
8. Sander Westerveld (v
Chelsea away)
9. John Scales
10. Neil Ruddock (18 October
1997 at Goodison Park)

32
**European Cup Winners
1983/84**

1. AS Roma
2. Odense Boldklub
3. Rome
4. 6–0 (Odense Boldklub
1–0 and 5–0)
5. FC Dinamo Bucureflti
6. Benfica
7. Athletic Club de Bilbao
8. Phil Neal

9. 69,693
10. Ian Rush, 5 goals

33
Terry McDermott
1. Newcastle United
2. 1974
3. 232
4. Newcastle United
5. Cork City FC
6. Athletic Football Club of Greeks of Nicosia (APOEL Nicosia)
7. Bury FC
8. 54
9. 1984
10. Newcastle United

34
Premiership Spot-Kick Scorers
1. Jan Molby (v Ipswich Town away on 25 August 1992)
2. Mark Walters
3. Tottenham Hotspur (at White Hart Lane)
4. Jari Litmanen
5. Patrik Berger (v Sunderland at Anfield on 11 March 2000)
6. Crystal Palace
7. Jamie Redknapp
8. Gary McAllister
9. Michael Owen
10. Danny Murphy

35
Elisha Scott
1. Goalkeeper
2. Belfast Celtic
3. 467
4. Northern Ireland and Republic of Ireland
5. 27
6. 1912
7. Linfield (Windsor Park)
8. 1934
9. Broadway United
10. Player-manager

36
The European Cup
1. Gerry Byrne (1964/65)
2. It was an own-goal by Austria Vienna's Obermayer on 20 March 1985
3. Juventus (1985 final)
4. Mark Lawrenson (24 April 1985)
5. Kenny Dalglish
6. 4
7. 1977
8. Ian Rush
9. 12
10. 159 (105 at home and 54 away)

37
John Barnes
1. Jamaica
2. 1987
3. Watford
4. 314
5. Newcastle United

6. Charlton Athletic
7. 84
8. Glasgow Celtic
9. Arsenal
10. The Jamaican national team

38
Jamie Carragher
1. The FA Youth Cup
2. The League (Coca-Cola) Cup
3. Middlesbrough
4. Aston Villa (18 January 1998)
5. Roy Evans
6. Hungary
7. Lucas Neil
8. Ian Callaghan
9. Luton Town (Liverpool won 5–0)
10. Inter Milan (at the Giuseppe Meazza Stadium)

39
Christmas Number Ones (I)
1. 'Earth Song'
2. Blue featuring Elton John
3. 2003
4. 'Caravan of Love'
5. 1991
6. Westlife
7. 1979
8. 'Ernie (the Fastest Milkman in the West)'
9. Jimmy Osmond
10. 1970

40
Nicknames (I)
1. Robbie Fowler
   God
2. Steve McManaman
   Shaggy
3. Neil Ruddock
   Razor
4. Emlyn Hughes
   Crazy Horse
5. Ron Yeats
   Rowdy
6. Kevin Keegan
   Mighty Mouse
7. Steve Heighway
   Big Bamber
8. John Barnes
   Digger
9. Fernando Morientes
   Nando
10. Tommy Smith
    Anfield Iron

41
Internationals (III)
1. Elisha Scott
2. Glenn Hysen
3. Finland
4. Abel Xavier
5. Igor Biscan
6. Martin Skrtel
7. David McMullen
8. Michael Owen
9. Dietmar Hamann and Christian Ziege
10. Brad Friedel

42
Former Away Grounds
1. Manchester City
2. Leicester City
3. Bolton Wanderers
4. Middlesbrough
5. Wimbledon
6. Brighton & Hove Albion
7. Coventry City
8. Southampton
9. Reading
10. Derby County

43
Fernando Torres
1. Madrid
2. The Nike Cup (1998)
3. Chelsea
4. Atletico Madrid
5. Portugal
6. Aston Villa (in a 2-1 win on 11 August 2007)
7. Chelsea (in a 1-1 draw on 19 August 2007)
8. The League (Carling) Cup (v Reading)
9. FC Porto
10. Germany

44
The Merseyside Derby (IV)
1. David Johnson
2. Peter Beardsley (Sandy Brown scored for both sides too with the Everton man scoring an own-goal as well as one for Everton during his career)
3. Steven Gerrard and Sander Westerveld (in a 3–2 Everton defeat)
4. Dirk Kuyt (for Liverpool in a 2–1 win at Goodison Park in the Premiership)
5. They won at Anfield for the first time and also won both derby games
6. Duncan Ferguson (4)
7. 1984/85 (1–0 in both First Division games)
8. Roy Vernon (1962), Wayne Clarke (1988) and David Unsworth (2001)
9. Robbie Fowler (6)
10. Season 1990/91 (a 4–4 draw and a 1–0 defeat)

45
Who Are We Playing? (I)
1. Arsenal
2. Brighton & Hove Albion
3. Barnsley
4. Barnet and Brentford
5. Accrington Stanley
6. Aston Villa
7. Burnley
8. Blackpool
9. Bristol Rovers
10. Burton Albion

46
League Champions 1983/84
1. 80
2. Wolverhampton Wanderers
3. Manchester United
4. Sunderland
5. 2
6. Ian Rush

7.   Norwich City
8.   West Bromwich Albion
9.   Ian Rush
10. 1

47
Players (I)

1.   Assistant Manager of the Norwegian national football team
2.   Jamie Carragher
3.   Phil Boersma
4.   Leeds United
5.   John Toshack
6.   Walsall
7.   Mark Walters
8.   Ray Clemence
9.   Charlton Athletic
10. Nigel Clough (Nottingham Forest)

48
Christmas Number Ones (II)

1.   'Lonely This Christmas'
2.   Band Aid
3.   2000
4.   'Mull of Kintyre'
5.   Human League
6.   1997
7.   'Do They Know It's Christmas?'
8.   Cliff Richard
9.   1982
10. 'Only You'

49
Ronnie Whelan

1.   Dublin
2.   Bob Paisley

3.   Stoke City
4.   Ray Kennedy
5.   The League Cup in season 1981/82
6.   6
7.   Alan Hansen
8.   The First Division League Championship in season 1989/90
9.   The FA Cup Final (Ronnie scored in the semi-final draw with Portsmouth)
10. Southend United

50
Domestic Cups 1983/84

1.   Brentford
2.   Fulham
3.   Birmingham City
4.   Sheffield Wednesday
5.   Walsall
6.   Everton
7.   Ian Rush
8.   Graeme Souness
9.   Newcastle United
10. Brighton & Hove Albion

51
Internationals (IV)

1.   Brad Friedel (USA)
2.   Rigobert Song (scored for Cameroon in 2000 final v Nigeria)
3.   2 (Jamie Carragher and Steven Gerrard)
4.   Manager of the Republic of Ireland football team
5.   0
6.   Jan Mølby (Denmark)

and Steve Nicol
(Scotland)
7. Steven Gerrard (scored 2
    for England)
8. Xabi Alonso (for Spain v
    Ukraine)
9. Brad Friedel (USA)
10. Kenny Dalglish (for
    Scotland v New Zealand)

52
Who Are We Playing? (II)
1. Bolton Wanderers
2. Cardiff City
3. Bournemouth
4. Carlisle United
5. Aldershot Town
6. Charlton Athletic
7. Coventry City
8. Bradford City
9. Chester City
10. Cambridge United

53
Away Days (II)
1. Bolton Wanderers
2. Crewe Alexandra
3. Brentford
4. Carlisle United
5. Bradford City
6. Charlton Athletic
7. Crystal Palace
8. Bristol City
9. Cheltenham Town
10. Canvey Island

54
Shirt Sponsors
1. Crown Paints
2. Canon
3. Umbro
4. Liverpool did not have a
    shirt sponsor in season
    1979/80
5. Carling
6. Barclays
7. Carlsberg
8. Reebok
9. Candy
10. Adidas

55
Reds at the World Cup (II)
1. Laurie Hughes (for
    England in 1950)
2. Kenny Dalglish and
    Graeme Souness
3. El Hadji Diouf, Dietmar
    Hamann, Jerzey Dudek,
    Emile Heskey and
    Michael Owen
4. Alan A'Court
5. Ian Callaghan (v France)
6. Alan Hansen (Scotland)
7. Paul Ince, Steve
    McManaman and
    Michael Owen
8. 4 (England, Germany,
    Poland and Senegal)
9. Harry Kewell (Australia)
10. Ray Houghton (Republic
    of Ireland)

56
Ian St John
1. Motherwell
2. 336
3. Coventry City
4. Everton
5. A hat-trick
6. Motherwell
7. 95
8. 1961
9. 21
10. Jimmy Greaves (*The Saint & Greavsie Show*)

57
Champions of Europe 2004/05
1. Grazer Athletik-Klub
2. AS Monaco
3. Olympiakos
4. Real Club Deportivo de La Coruña
5. TSV Bayer 04 Leverkusen e.V. Bayer 04 Leverkusen Fußball GmbH
6. Juventus (Liverpool lost the 1985 Final 1–0)
7. Chelsea
8. AC Milan
9. Liverpool 3 AC Milan 2
10. Steven Gerrard (he scored both goals in the Reds' 2–0 win over Grazer AK)

58
Mixed Bag (I)
1. Manchester United (won League game and lost FA Cup Final)

2. Milan Baros
3. Xabi Alonso
4. Julian Dicks
5. West Bromwich Albion
6. 9–9
7. Sunderland
8. 1983
9. A man pointed a gun at him
10. Both games finished 2–1 to the Reds and the same two players scored (Roger Hunt and Ian St John)

59
Who Are We Playing? (III)
1. Sunderland
2. Crewe Alexandra
3. Bristol City
4. Grimsby Town
5. Canvey Island
6. Fulham
7. Manchester City
8. Colchester United and Oxford United
9. Mansfield Town
10. Dagenham & Redbridge

60
European Championship Reds (II)
1. 0
2. 5
3. Ray Clemence, David Johnson, Ray Kennedy, Terry McDermott, Phil Neal and Phil Thompson
4. Ray Houghton (for Republic of Ireland v

England in 1988)
5. John Barnes
6. Robbie Fowler, Steve McManaman and Jamie Redknapp
7. 2
8. Stig Inge Bjørnebye and Vegard Heggem
9. 5
10. Patrik Berger and Vladimir Smicer

61
Nicknames (II)

1. David Johnson
   Doc
2. Tommy Lawrence
   The Flying Pig
3. Harry Chambers
   Smiler
4. Rob Jones
   Trigger
5. Brian Hall
   Little Bamber
6. Jason McAteer
   Dave
7. Harry Kewell
   The Wizard of Oz
8. Paul Ince
   The Guv'nor
9. Stan Collymore
   Stan the Man
10. Kenny Dalglish
    King Kenny

62
The Sporting Year (II)

1. 1985
2. 1966
3. 1989

4. 1984
5. 1998
6. 1986
7. 1987
8. 1995
9. 2002
10. 1983

63
Kenny Dalglish (II)

1. Glasgow Rangers
2. 7
3. 1978/79, 1979/80, 1981/82, 1982/83, 1983/84, 1985/86 and 1987/84
4. Cumbernauld United
5. £440,000
6. 1983
7. Pelé
8. 1989
9. Newcastle United
10. 6

64
Emlyn Hughes

1. 1967
2. 474
3. Hull City
4. Blackpool
5. 35
6. Defence
7. Wolverhampton Wanderers
8. Rotherham United
9. Melchester Rovers
10. 1979

ANSWERS

65
FA Cup Winners 1973/74
1. Newcastle United
2. Doncaster Rovers
3. John Toshack
4. Liverpool 3 Newcastle United 0
5. Leicester City
6. Bill Shankly
7. Bristol City
8. 3
9. Ipswich Town
10. Kevin Keegan (2), Steve Heighway

66
League Champions 1975/76
1. 60
2. Queens Park Rangers
3. Leeds United (3–0 on 26 August 1975)
4. Middlesbrough (0–2 at Anfield on 6 March 1976)
5. 14
6. John Toshack
7. Wolverhampton Wanderers (3–1 at Molineux)
8. Stoke City
9. Ian Callaghan
10. 5

67
Graeme Souness (I)
1. 1978
2. 247
3. Sampdoria
4. Middlesbrough
5. 38

6. Midfield
7. Glasgow Rangers
8. Galatasaray
9. 1991
10. Southampton

68
Phil Thompson (I)
1. 1971
2. 340
3. 18
4. Sheffield United
5. 7
6. Emlyn Hughes
7. Manchester United (a 3–0 win at Old Trafford on 3 April 1972)
8. Coach of Liverpool FC
9. Assistant manager
10. Winning the European Cup in 1981

69
UEFA Cup Winners 1975/76
1. FC Bruges
2. Hibernian
3. John Toshack (v Hibernian in a 3–1 Round 2, second-leg win)
4. Liverpool 4 FC Bruges 3
5. FC Barcelona
6. Bob Paisley
7. Dynamo Dresden
8. 1 (0–1 to Hibernian in Round 1, first leg)
9. Stask Wroclaw (3–0 at home and 2–1 away)
10. Kevin Keegan (2), Jimmy Case and Alan Kennedy

70
Who Are We Playing? (IV)

1. Lincoln City
2. West Bromwich Albion
3. Derby County
4. Doncaster Rovers
5. Huddersfield Town
6. Crystal Palace
7. Ipswich Town
8. Hartlepool United
9. Macclesfield Town
10. Gravesend & Northfleet

71
Gérard Houllier

1. Dundalk
2. 1998
3. Roy Evans
4. Paris Saint-Germain
5. The French national football team
6. Leeds United
7. The League Cup in season 2000/01
8. 2004 (24 May)
9. Olympique Lyonnais
10. The League Cup in season 2002/03

72
Players (II)

1. Emlyn Hughes
2. 3
3. Manchester United
4. 2004
5. Roger Hunt (5 goals)
6. Alec Lindsay
7. Stephen Warnock (v Birmingham City away)

8. Sydney Olympic FC
9. Middlesbrough
10. Brøndby IF

73
Mixed Bag (II)

1. Kenny Dalglish
2. Chelsea
3. 8
4. Crystal Palace and Everton
5. Left-back
6. Hercules CF
7. 2
8. 3
9. Phil Thompson (in 1981)
10. Chester City

74
Steve Heighway

1. Skelmersdale United
2. Dublin
3. Manchester United (on 3 April 1972 as a substitute in a 3–0 win)
4. 6
5. 50
6. 33 (with the Republic of Ireland)
7. 475
8. Coach of the Liverpool Academy
9. 5
10. 3

75
Rafael Benítez

1. Cantera (Real Madrid's youth team)

2. Castilla B
3. Valencia CF
4. Real Valladolid
5. Club Atlético Osasuna
6. AD Parla
7. The UEFA Champions League in 2004/05
8. CD Tenerife
9. Real Madrid
10. The UEFA Cup (with Valencia CF)

76
Reds at the World Cup (III)

1. Kenny Dalglish (for Scotland v Holland)
2. 0
3. Gary Gillespie
4. Jerzy Dudek (Poland)
5. 3 (Australia, England and Spain)
6. Ray Houghton, Steve Staunton and Ronnie Whelan
7. 0
8. Brad Friedel (USA)
9. 4 (England, Republic of Ireland, Spain and Sweden)
10. John Barnes, Peter Beardsley and Steve McMahon

77
The Trophy Years

1. 1981 – League Cup winners, European Cup winners
2. 1979 – First Division Champions, FA Charity Shield winners
3. 1992 – FA Cup winners
4. 1988 – First Division Champions, FA Charity Shield winners
5. 1986 – First Division Champions, FA Cup and Screen Sport Cup winners
6. 1982 – FA Charity Shield, League Cup, First Division Champions
7. 1984 – League Cup, First Division Champions, European Cup
8. 1976 – FA Charity Shield, First Division Champions, UEFA Cup
9. 1980 – FA Charity Shield, First Division Champions
10. 1977 – First Division Champions, European Cup, European Super Cup

---

78
Ray Clemence

1. 470
2. 1967
3. Scunthorpe United
4. 1970
5. Tottenham Hotspur
6. 21
7. 1981
8. Brazil
9. Doug Livermore
10. Prostate cancer

79
Past Masters (I)

1. 1978/79

2. Tranmere Rovers
3. Phil Neal
4. Lawro
5. Billy Liddell
6. Kevin Keegan and John Toshack
7. 12
8. Kolding Idrætsforening (Kolding IF)
9. He is the club's longest-serving player (he played for the Reds for 22 years)
10. Joey Jones

80
Liverpool's England Captains

1. Peter Beardsley
2. Hamburger SV
3. Sweden
4. Kevin Keegan
5. Phil Thompson
6. Mark Wright
7. 6
8. Paul Ince – Manchester United (2), Inter Milan (2) and Liverpool (3)
9. Phil Neal
10. Emlyn Hughes (on 11 May 1974 v Wales in a 2–0 England win)

81
Bruce Grobbelaar (I)

1. Vancouver Whitecaps
2. South Africa
3. Jim Beglin
4. Crewe Alexandra
5. Ray Clemence
6. The League Cup

(1981/82)
7. Stoke City (1992/93)
8. The *Sun*
9. Southampton
10. 440

82
Three Lions on a Shirt (I)

1. Tottenham Hotspur and Manchester United
2. Nick Barmby, Steven Gerrard, Emile Heskey and Michael Owen all started while Robbie Fowler (for Heskey) and Jamie Carragher (for Gerrard) came on as subs
3. Michael Owen
4. Alan A'Court
5. Philip Henry Taylor (1947)
6. Steven Gerrard
7. Tommy Smith
8. Gerald Byrne, James Melia and Gordon Milne
9. 6
10. Rabbi Howell

83
Away Days (III)

1. Fulham
2. Ipswich Town
3. Doncaster Rovers
4. Grimsby Town
5. Exeter City
6. York City
7. Leeds United
8. Gillingham
9. Leyton Orient
10. Darlington

84
Mark Lawrenson
1. Preston North End
2. Brighton & Hove Albion
3. 241
4. 1981
5. £900,000
6. 11
7. 1987
8. Republic of Ireland
9. A television football pundit (usually on *Football Focus*)
10. 39

85
Billy Liddell
1. Dunfermline (in Townhill on 10 January 1910)
2. Hamilton Academicals
3. George Kay
4. The RAF
5. Chester (in the 1946/47 FA Cup)
6. 534
7. Bob Paisley
8. The First Division Championship (1946/47)
9. 38
10. 1 (1950)

86
Phil Neal
1. 455
2. 1974
3. 23
4. Northampton Town
5. 41
6. 1985
7. First Division Championship (1985/86)
8. Bolton Wanderers
9. Chris Lawler
10. Cardiff City

87
Past Masters (II)
1. Carlisle United
2. 8
3. Phil Neal
4. Kevin Keegan
5. 0
6. Newcastle United
7. Jimmy Case
8. The European Cup (1978)
9. 1975
10. Terry McDermott

88
European Landmark Goals
1. Roger Hunt
2. Karl Heinz Riedle
3. Steve Heighway
4. Jimmy Case
5. Emlyn Hughes
6. Robbie Fowler
7. Alan Kennedy
8. Dean Saunders
9. Nick Barmby
10. Emile Heskey

89
Bob Paisley OBE
1. Physiotherapist
2. The FA Amateur Cup
3. Bishop Auckland
4. 1939
5. George Kay

6. 1946 (World War II delayed his Reds début until 5 January 1946)
7. 277
8. 1953/54
9. 1974
10. The 1974 FA Charity Shield

90
Steven Gerrard

1. 1998
2. Manchester United (he was a huge fan of the Manchester United and England captain Bryan Robson)
3. Number 4
4. Stevie G
5. MBE
6. Croatia
7. Number 17
8. Blackburn Rovers
9. George
10. Chelsea

91
The Reds' Welsh Dragons

1. John Toshack
2. 25
3. Joey Jones
4. 25
5. Dean Saunders (Aston Villa)
6. John Toshack
7. Joey Jones (Wrexham)
8. Swansea City
9. John Toshack
10. Ian Rush

92
The Merseyside Derby (V)

1. The 1989 FA Cup Final with the first of his 2 goals in the game
2. In memory of the 96 fans that had tragically lost their lives in the Hillsborough disaster on 15 April 1989
3. It was the last ever second replay in an FA Cup tie
4. 1897 (on 25 September 1897, Liverpool won the First Division encounter 3–1)
5. Elisha Scott
6. The Floodlit Challenge Cup (Liverpool won it 4 times and it can be seen today in their club museum)
7. Alan Hansen (the game ended 0–0)
8. Robbie Fowler
9. Alan Ball
10. Steve McMahon

93
Robbie Fowler

1. 1992
2. Cardiff City
3. Leeds United
4. Manchester City
5. 128
6. £11m
7. Everton
8. 26
9. Blackburn Rovers

10. The Top 1,000 Wealthiest Britons

94
Players (III)
1. Sammy Lee
2. Tommy Smith
3. Matt Busby
4. Jason McAteer (Head & Shoulders shampoo)
5. Arthur Riley (South Africa)
6. Peter Beardsley
7. Andy McGuigan 1901/02, John Evans 1954/55, Ian Rush 1983/84 and Robbie Fowler 1993/94
8. Steve Nicol
9. John Barnes (Watford lost 2–0 to Everton in 1984, Liverpool lost 1–0 to Wimbledon in 1988 and Newcastle United lost 2–0 to Arsenal in 1998)
10. Phil Thompson (versus Wales)

95
Mixed Bag (III)
1. Newcastle United
2. The BBC Sports Personality of the Year Team Award
3. John Wark
4. Luis Garcia (1–0 away win over Spurs on 30 December 2006)
5. Ephraim Longworth
6. The Shankly Gates

7. The Kop's Last Stand
8. Alan Hansen (1985/86)
9. Michael Owen, Emile Heskey and Jamie Carragher (Phil Neville of Manchester United was the fourth player)
10. Ian Callaghan

96
Awards (I)
1. Emlyn Hughes
2. Steve Ogrizovic
3. Bill Shankly
4. Bob Paisley
5. 1995 and 1996
6. Harry Kewell (Leeds United)
7. John Barnes
8. Michael Owen (2001)
9. Ian Rush (1983)
10. Kenny Dalglish

97
TV Stars
1. Kevin Keegan
2. Alan Hansen
3. Yosser Hughes
4. Bob Paisley
5. Emlyn Hughes (although Michael Owen captained a team for a single programme in February 2004)
6. Michael Owen
7. Bill Shankly
8. Kevin Keegan
9. Alan Hansen
10. Kenny Dalglish

98
Roy Evans

1. Defender
2. The North American Soccer League (with the Philadelphia Atoms)
3. Liverpool Reserves team manager
4. 5 (Bill Shankly, Bob Paisley, Joe Fagan, Kenny Dalglish and Graeme Souness)
5. Quintin Echlin
6. 1994
7. The League Cup in season 1994/95
8. Gérard Houllier
9. The Welsh national team (John Toshack was the manager)
10. Wrexham

99
Double Winners 1985/86 (I)

1. 88
2. Everton
3. Arsenal
4. White Hart Lane (Tottenham Hotspur)
5. Norwich City
6. Newcastle United (the Reds lost 1–0 away on 24 August 1985)
7. 6
8. Chelsea
9. Ian Rush (2) and Craig Johnston
10. Manchester City

100
John Toshack

1. Real Sociedad de Fútbol
2. 172
3. Cardiff City
4. 1970
5. 74
6. Swansea City
7. Wales
8. 12
9. Swansea City
10. Real Madrid

101
European Cup Winners 1977/78

1. FC Bruges
2. Dynamo Dresden
3. London (Wembley)
4. 5–1 (over Dynamo Dresden at Anfield)
5. Borussia Mönchengladbach
6. SL Benfica
7. 2
8. Jimmy Case (4)
9. Jimmy Case, Kenny Dalglish and Ray Kennedy
10. Bob Paisley

102
UEFA Cup Winners 1972/73

1. Borussia Mönchengladbach
2. Eintracht Frankfurt
3. Kevin Keegan (4)
4. Liverpool 3 Borussia Mönchengladbach 2

5. Tottenham Hotspur
6. Emlyn Hughes
7. Dynamo Dresden
8. 2
9. AEK Athens
10. Kevin Keegan (2) and Larry Lloyd

103
Almost Made It Six in 2006/07

1. Galatasaray
2. 4 (drew 1 and lost 1)
3. Bordeaux
4. FC Barcelona
5. 6
6. PSV Eindhoven
7. Chelsea
8. Liverpool 1 Chelsea 1 (Liverpool won the resulting penalty shootout)
9. Athens (Greece – Olympic Arena)
10. Dirk Kuyt

104
European Super Cup Winners

1. 3
2. 1977
3. Hamburger SV
4. David Fairclough (in a 1–1 away draw with Hamburger SV in the 1977 Final)
5. Stade Louis II, Monaco
6. Bayern Munich
7. CSKA Moscow (3–1 after extra-time)

8. John Arne Riise, Emile Heskey and Michael Owen
9. Luis Garcia (2005)
10. 1 (2001 – at the end of the 1998/99 season, the European Cup Winners' Cup was discontinued by UEFA and so, at the beginning of the 1999/2000 season, the European Super Cup was contested between the winners of the UEFA Champions League and the UEFA Cup)

105
Reds in print

1. *Over the Top – My Anfield Secrets* Tommy Smith
2. *Life at the Kop* Phil Neal
3. *A Matter of Opinion* Alan Hansen
4. *My Story* John Aldridge
5. *The Management Years* Graeme Souness
6. *Ray of Hope* Ray Kennedy
7. *My Soccer Story* Billy Liddell
8. *From Voikkaa to the Premiership* Sami Hyypia
9. *Ghosts on the Wall* Roy Evans
10. *Off the Record* Michael Owen

106
Testimonials
1. Jan Mølby
   PSV Eindhoven
2. Steve Heighway
   Everton
3. Bill Shankly
   Don Revie XI
4. Billy Liddell
   International XI
5. Ian St John   Chelsea
6. Ian Rush
   Glasgow Celtic
7. Ronnie Whelan
   Newcastle United
8. Ian Callaghan
   Lancashire XI
9. Sammy Lee Osasuna
10. Emlyn Hughes
    Borussia
    Mönchengladbach

107
League Cup Winners (I)
1. 7
2. 1981
3. 1978
4. Alan Kennedy
   (1981 Final)
5. 2003
6. Manchester United
7. Graeme Souness
8. 1994/95
9. Emlyn Hughes
   (with Wolverhampton
   Wanderers in the 1980
   final)
10. 2005

108
Ron Yeats
1. Aberdeen
2. Dundee United
3. 1961
4. £30,000
5. Bill Shankly
6. Tranmere Rovers
7. 454
8. The Second Division
   Championship (1961/62)
9. 16
10. 1971

109
Players (IV)
1. Phil Neal
2. Emlyn Hughes, Chris
   Lawler, Larry Lloyd and
   Tommy Smith
3. Spain
4. 1
5. Xabi Alonso
6. Achilles tendon damage
7. He is England's tallest
   player (6ft 7in)
8. Michael Owen
9. Kenny Dalglish
10. Jack Balmer (on 9
    November 1946 Liverpool
    beat Portsmouth 3–0; on
    16 November 1946 the
    Reds beat Derby County
    4–1 and on 23 November
    1946 Liverpool beat
    Arsenal 4–2

110
Mixed Bag (IV)
1. 'You'll Never Walk Alone'
2. AC Milan (4)
3. Robbie Fowler (Sheffield United away on the opening day)
4. Jock Stein
5. The FA Charity Shield
6. Jeremy Goss (Norwich City won 1–0)
7. Liverpool 1 Everton 0
8. Bob Paisley
9. Aston Villa (64), Tottenham Hotspur (59), Arsenal (57) and Everton (57) – Liverpool (54)
10. West Ham

111
For the Record
1. Djibril Cissé (£14m from Auxerre in July 2004)
2. He is Liverpool's oldest débutant, débuting against Burton United on 1 September 1904, aged 37 years and 307 days
3. Roger Hunt
4. Ian Rush
5. Billy Liddell
6. Liverpool 11 Stromsgodset (Norway) 0
7. The European Cup Winners' Cup (on 17 September 1974 at Anfield)
8. Gordon Hodgson
9. £12.5m for Robbie Fowler in November 2001

10. Wolverhampton Wanderers in the fourth round of the FA Cup on 2 February 1952

112
Away Days (IV)
1. West Bromwich Albion
2. Queens Park Rangers
3. Rotherham United
4. Scarborough
5. West Ham United
6. Reading
7. Scunthorpe
8. Rochdale
9. Southport
10. Kidderminster Harriers

113
Tommy Smith
1. 1962
2. Swansea City
3. 467
4. 1978
5. 4
6. Foot injury caused by a DIY accident
7. Ron Yeats
8. 638
9. The League and UEFA Cup Double
10. Number 10

114
Kenny Dalglish (III)
1. John Barnes
2. The Quality Street Gang
3. 1970, 1971, 1972, 1973, 1974 and 1977

4. 2 (1970 and 1975)
5. 1975
6. 3
7. 1978, 1981 and 1984
8. Blackburn Rovers
9. Joe Fagan
10. 1985/86

115
Graeme Souness (II)

1. Torino Calcio
2. Benfica
3. Newcastle United
4. Tottenham Hotspur
5. Montreal Olympique
6. 3
7. Jock Wallace
8. 3
9. Terry Butcher
10. The Scottish League Cup

116
Phil Thompson (II)

1. 1979
2. Bob Paisley
3. 43
4. A Reserve Team
    Championship winners'
    medal
5. Larry Lloyd
6. 1 (v Italy in New York
    City 1975/76)
7. Malcolm Macdonald
8. Don Revie
9. Ray Clemence, Kevin
    Keegan, Ray Kennedy
    and Phil Neal
10. 7

117
Internationals (V)

1. Nicolas Anelka, Bruno
    Cheyrou, Djibril Cissé
    and Alou Diarra
2. Arthur Riley
3. Salif Diao and El Hadji
    Diouf
4. Finnish
5. Jerzy Dudek
6. Zimbabwe
7. Stig Bjornebye, Vegard
    Heggem, Oyvind
    Leonhardsen and John
    Arne Riise
8. Dean Saunders
9. Edward and Maurice
    Parry
10. Joey Jones

118
Bill Shankly OBE

1. Preston North End
2. Carlisle United
3. Liverpool Reserves
4. Partick Thistle
5. 1959 (on 1 December)
6. Huddersfield Town
7. The Second Division
    Championship (1961/62)
8. 2 (1965/66 and 1972/73)
9. The European Cup
    Winners' Cup Final
10. Jack Charlton

119
Players (V)

1. Peter Beardsley (he played
    6 League games for Man
    City in 1998 on loan)

2. He is the youngest player to play for the club, making his sole appearance against Tottenham Hotspur on 8 May 1974, aged 17 years and 129 days

3. Newcastle United (in a 2–0 win at Anfield on 20 September 2006)

4. Roger Hunt

5. Ray Clemence and Brian Hall

6. Ron Yeats

7. 2001

8. Phil Neal

9. Rigobert Song

10. Dietmar Hamann (in a 1–0 win for Germany against England on 7 October 2000)

120
Mixed Bag (V)

1. Emlyn Hughes

2. Liverpool (1905 & 1906), Everton (1931 & 1932), Tottenham Hotspur (1950 & 1951) and Ipswich Town (1961 & 1962)

3. Joe Fagan

4. Real Madrid

5. Phil Neal

6. 2 (European Cup Winners' Cup 1965/66 and UEFA Cup 1972/73)

7. The Sherpa Van Trophy

8. Ian Rush

9. Roger Hunt (he scored four times in England's 10–0 win over the USA in New York on 27 May 1964)

10. 22

121
Bruce Grobbelaar (II)

1. 1981

2. Zimbabwe

3. Jomo Cosmos

4. John Fashanu and Hans Segers

5. *More Than Somewhat*

6. Seven Stars

7. Zimbabwe

8. The FA Cup (1991/92)

9. Greece

10. 1994

122
Three Lions on a Shirt (II)

1. Gordon Hodgson (3 caps 1930/31)

2. Manchester United (951) Liverpool (835)

3. Roger Hunt (1962)

4. 6

5. Ray Clemence, David Johnson, Phil Neal and Phil Thompson all started while Ray Kennedy (for Johnson) and Terry McDermott came on as subs

6. 6

7. 105

8. Ian Callaghan, Ray Clemence, Emlyn Hughes (captain), Ray Kennedy, Terry

McDermott and Phil Neal (Kevin Keegan, of SV Hamburg, also started)
9. He was the first black player to captain the England senior side
10. Kevin Keegan

123
Alan Hansen
1. Partick Thistle
2. 434
3. 1977
4. 8
5. 1990
6. On the BBC's Saturday-night TV show *Match of the Day*
7. 22
8. £100,000
9. 26
10. Derby County (a 1–0 win for the Reds on 24 September 1977)

124
European Cup Winners 1980/81
1. Real Madrid
2. Oulu Palloseura
3. Paris
4. Liverpool 10 Oulu Palloseura 1
5. Bayern Munich
6. CSKA Sofia
7. 0
8. Graeme Souness
9. Ray Kennedy
10. Alan Kennedy

125
Roger Hunt
1. The Second Division Championship (1961/62)
2. 1959
3. 492
4. 34
5. 286
6. 2000
7. Sir Roger
8. Bolton Wanderers
9. Scunthorpe United (Liverpool won 2–0)
10. 1969

126
Liverpool's Cup Treble (I)
1. 2000/01
2. Arsenal
3. FC Barcelona
4. Robbie Fowler
5. Vladimir Smicer
6. Rapid Bucharest (Round 1, 1–0 at home and 0–0 away)
7. Stoke City
8. Emile Heskey (5 goals)
9. Babbel, Gerrard, McAllister (pen) and Fowler (plus an OG)
10. Villa Park

127
FA Cup Winners 1991/92
1. Sunderland
2. Crewe Alexandra (4–0 away)
3. Michael Thomas
4. Liverpool 2 Sunderland 0

5. Arsenal (Arsenal Stadium)
6. Graeme Souness
7. Ipswich Town
8. Dean Saunders
9. Steve MacManaman
10. Ian Rush and Michael Thomas

128
League Champions 1989/90
1. 79
2. Manchester City
3. Derby County (3–0 on 9 September 1989)
4. John Barnes (including a penalty)
5. 13
6. John Barnes
7. Coventry City
8. Nottingham Forest
9. Liverpool 9 Crystal Palace 0
10. Millwall

129
The Champions
1. 1900–1910 (Champions in 1900/01)
2. 6
3. Bob Paisley (6)
4. 1963/64
5. 4
6. 1946/47
7. 1904/05 and 1905/06
8. Tom Watson
9. 3 (Bob Paisley, Joe Fagan and Kenny Dalglish)

10. 1893/94, 1895/96, 1904/05 and 1961/62

130
Cup Mixture
1. Derby County (0–1 at the Baseball Ground)
2. Jimmy Case
3. 2
4. Bolton Wanderers (1–0 away in Round 5)
5. Alan Kennedy and Terry McDermott
6. Round 2 (after a replay)
7. Real Sociedad
8. Luton Town 3 Liverpool 5
9. 2 (1964/65 and 1973/74)
10. Arsenal

131
Mixed Bag (VI)
1. 1974
2. Nicolas Anelka (Arsenal)
3. Gary Neville
4. Oxford United
5. Alvin Martin
6. 1980/81
7. Old Trafford
8. Willie Stevenson
9. John Toshack
10. 8

132
League Champions 1987/88
1. 90
2. Arsenal
3. Everton (a) and Nottingham Forest (a)
4. Luton Town

5. 20
6. John Aldridge
7. Oxford United
8. Wimbledon
9. 5–0 (against Nottingham Forest at Anfield on 13 April 1988)
10. 4

133
FA Cup Winners 1988/89

1. Everton
2. Carlisle United
3. Nottingham Forest
4. Liverpool 3 Everton 2 (after extra time)
5. John Aldridge
6. Kenny Dalglish
7. Hull City
8. Old Trafford
9. Brentford
10. John Aldridge

134
Liverpool's Cup Treble (II)

1. CD Alaves
2. Michael Owen
3. Rotherham United (3–0 at Anfield)
4. Birmingham City (5–4 on penalties after a 1–1 draw)
5. AS Roma (won 2–0 away and lost 1–0 at Anfield)
6. Wycombe Wanderers
7. Borussia Dortmund (Westfalenstadion or Signal Iduna Park)
8. Nick Barmby
9. Crystal Palace

10. 25 (6 FA Cup, 6 League Cup and 13 UEFA Cup)

135
League Cup Winners (II)

1. Old Trafford (1–0 to Nottingham Forest in the 1978 replay)
2. Nottingham Forest
3. West Ham United (1981, 2–1 in a replay after a 1–1 draw)
4. 1984 (season 1983/84)
5. Villa Park (1981)
6. Tottenham Hotspur
7. Bolton Wanderers
8. Chelsea
9. Roy Evans (1995)
10. Maine Road (Manchester City)

136
World Club Championship

1. 0
2. 3
3. 1981
4. Flamengo (1981)
5. Tokyo, Japan (National Stadium)
6. 0
7. Borussia Mönchengladbach (1977 European Cup runners-up to the Reds)
8. They could not agree the two necessary fixture dates with their South American opponents
9. Boca Juniors
10. Sao Paulo

137
League Champions 1972/73
1. 60
2. Manchester City
3. Sheffield United (5–0 at Anfield on 23 September 1972)
4. Newcastle United
5. Arsenal (0–2)
6. Kevin Keegan
7. Leicester City
8. West Ham United (1–0 win at Upton Park on 6 January 1973)
9. Brian Hall
10. John Toshack

138
Double Winners 1985/86 (II)
1. Kenny Dalglish (player-manager)
2. Everton (the Reds lost 2–0 at Anfield on 22 February 1986)
3. Southampton (2–0)
4. 16
5. Jan Mølby
6. Ian Rush
7. Norwich City
8. York City
9. 6
10. Kenny Dalglish (in a 1–0 away win at Chelsea)

139
Awards (II)
1. Bob Paisley
2. Michael Owen (1998)
3. Ian Rush
4. Kenny Dalglish

5. John Barnes
6. Paul Walsh
7. Kevin Keegan
8. Bob Paisley, Kenny Dalglish, Kevin Keegan and Bill Shankly
9. Terry McDermott (1980)
10. 1998

140
The Welsh Connection
1. None
2. Cardiff City
3. 3 (and 1 draw)
4. Wrexham
5. Geoff Hurst
6. Brazil
7. Wrexham
8. 39
9. 0
10. 5

141
UEFA Champions League Glory 2004/05
1. Grazer UK
2. AS Monaco
3. Olympiacos (1–0 in Athens on Matchday Two)
4. Deportivo de La Coruña
5. Bayer Leverkusen
6. Sami Hyypia and Luis Garcia
7. Istanbul (Turkey – the Ataturk Stadium)
8. Chelsea
8. Steven Gerrard, Vladimir Smicer and Xabi Alonso
10. John Arne Riise (Dietmar

Hamann, Djibril Cisse
and Vladimir Smicer all
scored)

142
Joe Fagan

1. Bob Paisley
2. 1983/84
3. Liverpool (on 12 March 1921)
4. Nelson FC
5. 1958
6. The FA Charity Shield
7. The League Cup and the European Cup
8. 1 (1983/84)
9. Manchester City
10. 1984/85

143
The Premiership Years (II)

1. It was the 200th (it was also the 99th meeting between the two sides at Goodison and the 25th meeting in the FA Premier League)
2. Nick Barmby (Tottenham Hotspur, Middlesbrough, Everton, Liverpool, Leeds United) and Stan Collymore (Nottingham Forest, Liverpool, Aston Villa, Leicester City, Bradford City). The others are: Les Ferdinand (6 clubs – QPR, Newcastle United, Tottenham Hotspur, West Ham United, Leicester City and Bolton Wanderers); Andy Cole (6 clubs – Newcastle United, Manchester United, Fulham, Blackburn Rovers, Manchester City, Portsmouth); Benito Carbone (Sheffield Wednesday, Villa, Bradford, Middlesbrough, Derby County); Mark Hughes (Manchester United, Chelsea, Everton, Blackburn Rovers, Southampton); Teddy Sheringham (Nottingham Forest, Tottenham Hotspur, Manchester United, Portsmouth, West Ham United); Ashley Ward (Norwich City, Derby County, Barnsley, Blackburn Rovers, Bradford City)
3. Nick Barmby (he left Everton for Liverpool three months earlier claiming he loved Liverpool more than Everton)
4. Aston Villa and Charlton Athletic (Liverpool and Northampton Town are the only other clubs of the 92 in the English Premiership/Football League in season 2008/09 whose names begin and end with the same letter)
5. Twix
6. Arsenal, Aston Villa, Chelsea, Everton, Manchester United and Tottenham Hotspur
7. Portsmouth (255 miles,

the shortest away journey was the short walk across Stanley Park to Goodison Park)

8. Mark Clattenburg (Everton were unhappy with the referee for sending off Tony Hibbert yet only booked Liverpool's Dirk Kuyt for a dangerously high two-footed lunge at Phil Neville)

9. Arsenal (2)

10. Arsenal (Arsenal Stadium and Emirates Stadium), Bolton Wanderers (Burnden Park and Reebok Stadium), Derby County (Baseball Ground and Pride Park Stadium), Leicester City (Filbert Street and Walkers Stadium), Manchester City (Maine Road and Eastlands), Middlesbrough (Ayresome Park and Riverside Stadium), Southampton (The Dell and St Mary's) and Sunderland (Roker Park and Stadium of Light) – Wimbledon never played at Plough Lane in the Premiership as they used Selhurst Park

---

144
Internationals (VI)

1. Kevin Keegan (England)
2. Graeme Souness
3. Jan Mølby

4. John Toshack
5. Emlyn Hughes
6. 3
7. Robert Matthews (WWI), Ray Lambert (WWII) and G Poland (WWII)
8. 1
9. Billy Liddell
10. Cameroon

145
Graeme Souness (III)

1. 54
2. East Germany
3. Liverpool
4. 5
5. Edinburgh (on 6 May 1953)
6. Celtic
7. 4
8. 2
9. Blackburn Rovers
10. Sir Bobby Robson

146
FA Cup Winners 2005/06

1. West Ham United
2. Portsmouth
3. He scored it from his own half
4. Liverpool 3 West Ham 3
5. Chelsea
6. Steven Gerrard (v Luton Town in Round 3)
7. Birmingham City
8. Hamann, Hyypia, Gerrard, Riise
9. Manchester United
10. Old Trafford

147
Christmas Number Ones (III)

1. '(Just Like) Starting Over'
2. Take That
3. 1973
4. 'Somethin' Stupid'
5. 'Bohemian Rhapsody'
6. 1988
7. 'I Will Always Love You'
8. Dunblane
9. 1976
10. Boney M

148
Who Are We Playing? (V)

1. Manchester United
2. Luton Town
3. Exeter City
4. Leyton Orient
5. Grays Athletic
6. Portsmouth
7. Millwall
8. Milton Keynes
9. Northampton Town
10. Halifax Town

149
The Merseyside Derby (VI)

1. Liverpool is the only city to have staged top-flight football in every League season since the Football League began in season 1888/89
2. Birmingham (Aston Villa, Birmingham City and West Bromwich Albion), Bristol (City and Rovers), London (numerous), Manchester (City and United), Nottingham (County and Forest), Sheffield (United and Wednesday) and Stoke (Stoke City and Port Vale)
3. Peter Beardsley
4. Steve McMahon
5. William 'Dixie' Dean
6. Robbie Fowler
7. Liverpool 0 Everton 2
8. Dave Watson
9. 1986 (on 29 January in a 3–0 away win over Egypt)
10. Liverpool 1 Everton 0

150
Kenny Dalglish (IV)

1. 1991
2. 1999
3. 2 (1979 and 1983)
4. 1983
5. 1975/76
6. Belgium
7. Jock Stein
8. Archie Gemmill
9. 1998
10. Glasgow Celtic

REFERENCES

Publications

The Liverpool Football Miscellany, by John White, Carlton Publishing Group (2006)

Liverpool in Europe, by Ivan Ponting and Steve Hall with Steve Small and Alex Murphy, Carlton Publishing Group (2005)

The Official Liverpool Illustrated Encyclopedia, by Jeff Anderson with Stephen Done, Carlton Publishing Group (2003)

Liverpool FC – The Historic Treble, Carlton Publishing Group (2001)

The Official Liverpool Illustrated History Second Edition, by Jeff Anderson with Stephen Done, Carlton Publishing Group (2003)

The Official Bolton Wanderers Quiz Book, by Marc White, Apex Publishing Limited (2008)

Useful Websites

http://www.liverweb.org.uk

http:// www.liverpool.rivals.net

http://www.liverpoolfc.tv

http://www.guardian.co.uk/football

http://www.lfc4life.com

http://www.lfconline.com

http://en.wikipedia.org

http://icliverpool.icnetwork.co.uk

http://www.lfcbootroom.net

http://www.shankly.com

http://www.lfchistory.net